Instructor's Resource Manual

to accompany

P.O.W.E.R. Learning and Your Life

Essentials of Student Success

First Edition

Robert S. Feldman
University of Massachusetts-Amherst

Prepared by
Cindy Wallace
Joni Webb Petschauer
both of Appalachian State University

Connect
Learn
Succeed™

Instructor's Resource Manual to accompany
P.O.W.E.R. Learning and Your Life: Essentials of Student Success
Robert S. Feldman

Published by McGraw-Hill, a business unit of The McGraw-Hill Companies, Inc., 1221 Avenue of the Americas, New York, NY 10020. Copyright © 2011 by The McGraw-Hill Companies, Inc.
All rights reserved.

1 2 3 4 5 6 7 8 9 0 WDD/WDD 1 0 9 8 7 6 5 4 3 2 1 0

ISBN   978-0-07-742965-2
MHID   0-07-742965-6

www.mhhe.com

Dedicated to Appalachian State University's instructors of first year students

Your commitment to teaching makes a difference to the lives of our students.

CONTENTS

PREFACE

". . . as I packed my belongings and prepared to make the leap into this abyss known as "the real world," I could not help but reflect upon my years at Appalachian. . . . My first semester included your Freshman Seminar class. The most important part of that semester was not so much the curriculum, but the way you taught that class. From the first day, you treat students as peers, not as subjects. Further, your class was about learning to think independently and critically. In short, it was about learning to learn about yourself and the world around you. I have come to realize that we must understand certain things about ourselves before we can really understand the rest of the world. I think that you were one of the first people that really made me see how wide open the world really is. Although at the time I thought I had a plan from which I would never stray, the realm of possibility that exists during one's college years was (and continues to be) a revelation. The idea that life has a thousand things to offer and you have only to choose a path is one that you introduced to us, and later years have reinforced in me."

Letter from Stephen Vinson to Cindy Wallace

Stephen's letter explains why we teach. His experience is what we hope to provide for every student we meet. It is an honor to witness the self-discovery and personal awareness that accompanies a rigorous and thoughtful academic journey. But we seldom know if we hit the mark because learning is not always joyful or inspiring. In fact, sometimes, it gets downright messy and more often than not, extremely uncomfortable. Yet, when we stay with it, and genuinely commit ourselves to moving beyond the surface issues and the easy stuff, we all—students and faculty—learn to be better citizens, parents, partners, and friends than we ever thought we could be. That is why we teach.

DESIGN OF THE INSTRUCTOR'S MANUAL

We are so very pleased to have been asked to continue working with the folks at McGraw-Hill on the first edition of *P.O.W.E.R. Learning and Your Life: Essentials of Student Success.* Without a doubt, being affiliated with the committed and professional individuals of that special company continues to be one of our most rewarding life experiences. And, after many years of teaching first year students, we found it exciting to try and put into words our love for working with them, our commitment to the value of higher education and our belief in the significance of good teaching, from the moment a student chooses to embark on this journey.

Another compelling reason for writing the Instructor's Manual for this edition was the chance to continue to work with and learn from someone like Bob Feldman. The breadth and depth of his teaching and his wonderful way of connecting with students led him to write what we consider to be the very best student success book available today. This edition of *P.O.W.E.R. Learning and Your Life: Essentials of Student Success* has been thoughtfully written to include the variety of students and institutions engaged in post-secondary education. It includes important ideas such as expected learning outcomes for each chapter, compelling reasons to change habits, information about technology and information competency, and questions geared towards developing critical thinking skills in the Journal Reflections. References to the challenges faced by students who work, attend schools, and have families are abundant throughout the text. Feldman personalizes his conversation with students and we are sure that they will appreciate his timely ideas about the world in which they live and learn. What we intuitively believe are good teaching practices works well with and are supported by the P.O.W.E.R. rubric set forth in his text. Included in this manual is a section on "The Research Basis for P.O.W.E.R. Learning" in which Feldman connects the systematic approach to student success to current educational literature. It is definitely worth reading.

We have tried to use a framework similar to Feldman's in the way we have structured our own work in the Instructor's Manual. Our goals are stated in the first section and our basic premise is a reflection of Feldman's—good instructors (like good students) are made, not born. It is something we must work at every day. Just as Feldman suggests strategies to make students more successful, we propose strategies for making instructors more successful.

We begin our discussion of good teaching and successful freshman seminar/success courses with "Course Development and Classroom Management Tips." This section provides suggestions for course goals and course content, includes syllabi examples, teaching techniques, assessment and evaluation information, as well as tips from experienced faculty.

For those of you who are establishing student success courses on your campus or are in the midst of enhancing your program, we have included "Implications for Broader Faculty Development on Your Campus." McGraw-Hill has resources that can assist you in developing and sustaining your student success course and you should ask your representative about these supports. Also included are materials to help sustain your course through faculty development programs and online resources. Our goal is to provide you with ideas about recruiting and training faculty for this course while promoting broader campus-wide efforts to ensure student success.

The heart of this manual is found in "Teaching the Text." This section includes chapter-by-chapter notes that are organized in the following way:

I.   Chapter Summary–A *Message to the student* and a *Message to the instructor* provide a focused introduction to each chapter.

II.   Ideas and Concepts to Consider–Includes key concepts from the text as well as a few which may extend the conceptual framework.

III.   Clarifying Questions and Discussion Prompts–Provides a starting point for class discussion, small group work, and/or individual reflection about the information presented in each chapter.

IV.   Classroom Activities and Assignments–Encourages the use of exercises and activities when teaching each chapter. We also have references when these teaching activities are included in the Annotated Instructor's Edition.

V.   Using the P.O.W.E.R. Learning Process in Your Instruction–Whether you are learning to learn or learning to teach (or teach better!), Feldman's *P.O.W.E.R. Learning* process is a useful tool. Here are our ideas for applying this process as an instructor with each chapter.

VI.   Continuing the Conversation beyond the Classroom–Suggests ways for instructors to create opportunities for students to connect the course content to the individual student's life, the broader practices and programs in the academic community, and the world in which we live–our global society.

VII.   Classroom Activities to Support Teaching This Chapter–Rather than put activities in an appendix, we have placed them with each chapter to provide opportunities to make the learning process an active one.

In addition to this manual, McGraw-Hill provides first-rate teaching aids including the Annotated Instructor's Edition and a number of on-line resources at: **www.mhhe.com/power** that we encourage you to use. As noted in the preface of Feldman's text, these materials were developed in conjunction with practiced faculty who know what is needed to teach an excellent student success course. These resources include:

PRINT RESOURCES

P.O.W.E.R. Learning and Your Life: Essentials of Student Success, **1st edition (0-07-337520-9).** Written by Bob Feldman of University of Massachusetts at Amherst, this textbook is a provocative and thoughtful guide for students beginning their college education. Feldman's stories of academic success and up-to-date exercises engage students in a genuine journey of intellectual self-reflection.

Annotated Instructor's Edition (AIE) (0-07-737539-4). The AIE, prepared by Joni Webb Petschauer and Cindy Wallace of Appalachian State University, contains the full text of the student edition of the book with the addition of marginal notes that provide a rich variety of teaching strategies, discussion prompts, and helpful cross-references to the Instructor's Manual.

Customize Your Text P.O.W.E.R. Learning can be customized to suit your needs. The text can be abbreviated for shorter courses and can be expanded to include semester schedules, campus maps, additional essays, activities, or exercises, along with other materials specific to your curriculum or situation. Chapters designed for student athletes, transferring students, and careers are also available.

Distance Learning Faculty Guide: Designing and Teaching a Distance Learning Course with P.O.W.E.R. Learning, written by Christopher Poirier and Robert S. Feldman, will provide instructors with an overview of distance learning, an introduction to the most popular distance learning platforms, and detailed instructions on how to design and teach a distance-learning course with *P.O.W.E.R. Learning*.

HUMAN RESOURCES

Workshops with Author and Author Team: Are you faced with the challenge of launching a first-year experience course on your campus? Would you like to invigorate your college success program, incorporating the most recent pedagogical and technological innovations? Is faculty recruitment an obstacle to the success of your program? Are you interested in learning more about the P.O.W.E.R. system? Workshops are available on these and many other subjects for anyone conducting or even just considering a first-year experience program. Led by author Robert Feldman, P.O.W.E.R. Learning Instructor's Manual authors Joni Webb Petschauer and Cindy Wallace, or one of the McGraw-Hill *P.O.W.E.R. Learning* consultants, each workshop is tailored to the needs of individual campuses or programs. For more information, contact your local representative, or drop us a line at **fye@mcgraw-hill.com**.

DIGITAL RESOURCES

McGraw-Hill Connect Plus+: Connect Plus+ includes powerful tools and features that allow students to access their coursework anytime and anywhere, while you control assignments. Connect Plus+ provides students with their textbook and homework, all in one accessible place. McGraw-Hill provides live instructor orientations for Connect Plus+ to guarantee you will have a worry-free experience.

LASSI: Learning and Study Strategies Inventory: The LASSI is a 10-scale, 80-item assessment of students' awareness about and use of learning and study strategies related to skill, will, and self-regulation components of strategic learning. The focus is on covert and overt thoughts, behaviors, attitudes, and beliefs that relate to successful learning and that can be altered through educational interventions. Research has repeatedly demonstrated that these factors contribute significantly to success in college and that they can be learned or enhanced through educational interventions such as learning and study skills courses.

The LASSI provides standardized scores and national norms for ten different scales. The LASSI is both diagnostic and prescriptive. It provides students with a diagnosis of their strengths and weaknesses compared to other college students in the areas covered by the 10 scales, and it is prescriptive in that it provides feedback about areas where students may be weak and need to improve their knowledge, attitudes, beliefs, and skills. The LASSI is available in print or online at **www.hhpublishing.com**. Ask your McGraw-Hill sales representative for more details.

P.O.W.E.R. Learning Web Site (www.mhhe.com/power): Instructors and students will find downloadable resources, demonstrations of all of our software programs, opportunities for online discussion, e-mail access to the author and project contributors, Web exercises, transparency masters, and a rich bank of links for college success.

PowerText: Available free with the purchase of a new text, this online resource provides an integrated learning experience that combines the traditional content of the textbook with the media-rich environment of the Internet. See pages xxiv through xxvii for a visual tour of this exciting product.

PageOut, WebCT, Blackboard, and more: The online content of *P.O.W.E.R. Learning* is supported by WebCT, eCollege.com, and Blackboard. Additionally, our PageOut service, free to qualified adopters, is available to get you and your course up and running online in a matter of hours! To find out more contact your local McGraw-Hill representative or visit **www.pageout.net**.

*****

Each semester of teaching marks a new journey in learning. Our goal is to provide you with ideas that can be taken in various directions by you and your students. We invite you to contact us if you have questions or concerns and especially when you want to celebrate your successes. We promise to respond. Good luck and best wishes!

Joni Webb Petschauer
Director, Western NC Network
    for Access and Success
Appalachian State University
Boone, North Carolina 28608
828-262-3878
E-mail: **petschaerjw@appstate.edu**

Cindy Wallace
Vice Chancellor
    for Student Development
Appalachian State University
Boone, North Carolina 28608
828-262-2060
E-mail: **wallaceca@appstate.edu**

ACKNOWLEDGMENTS

As our work on this edition comes to an end, we find ourselves so very grateful to the many hands and hearts that have made the book a reality. Opportunities for publicly thanking those who have supported our accomplishments come too seldom in life and so, even at the risk of inadvertently leaving someone out, we wish to take time to express our appreciation.

First, our institution, Appalachian State University, has over a hundred years of engaging students in the academic community. It is a dynamic and ever-changing place but it has always placed a high priority on the importance of undergraduate education. It is important to us to acknowledge the many faculty, staff, and students who have shouldered this work and made our efforts easier. We particularly wish to thank the many individuals for their collective support and individual contributions to the Freshman Seminar program and student success efforts at Appalachian. Their work lives on in the decisions of those who have followed. Our current Chancellor, Ken Peacock continues to support the program wholeheartedly. Dr. Dave Haney and Dr. Lynn Moss Sanders lead the First Year Seminar program on the Appalachian campus and through the curricular leadership efforts of Provost Stan Aeschleman, the course is now integrated into Appalachian's general education and required for all students. Together they inspire teachers to take the necessary risks on behalf of their students.

Student success is a shared agenda on the Appalachian campus and is an excellent example of how a partnership between Academic Affairs and Student Affairs can improve the learning that can be achieved. The evolution of Appalachian's course from Freshman Seminar to First Year Seminar has intentionally included all parts of the campus in its attempt to support students and has developed a reputation for innovation and inclusion. Faculty, staff, and students come together to create, explore, learn, and grow. It is our genuine hope that our colleagues and students feel honored by our sharing their ideas, classroom activities, and suggestions in this book. From them we have learned "what works."

Our work with McGraw-Hill's *P.O.W.E.R. Learning* team over these past years has expanded and enriched our understanding of collaboration and teamwork. We consider ourselves incredibly fortunate to be supported by an endless group of talented professionals: Alice Harrah, Keari Green, Kristin Bradley, and Gary O'Brien are professional, knowledgeable and forthright. Additionally, McGraw-Hill has allowed us the opportunity to meet and learn from like-minded educators from around the country and we are grateful for their input. Finally, we want thank those individuals who patiently guided our efforts on earlier editions. They remain important to our thinking and working about this project: Sarah Touberg, Rhona Robbin, Andy Watts, Alexis Walker, Mary Conzachi, Ken Guerin, Bob Oakley, Ben Morrison, Katie Pascali, Leslie Oberhuber, Lisa Berry, Lake Lloyd, David Patterson, Beth Mejia, Phil Butcher, Thalia Dorwick, and Steve Dubow. McGraw-Hill's commitment to student success extends far beyond this text and its ancillaries. They have sponsored individualized workshops, forums and the Institute for Student Success and Academic Change (ISSAC), giving faculty, administrators, and institutional teams from around the nation an opportunity to identify concerns related to student learning.

A special thanks goes to Bob Feldman. We consider him our wisest conversation partner. Whether it is an early morning e-mail response to a question, responding to a call to be a speaker on a campus, or taking notes on a napkin at a restaurant, he always brings a disciplined mind and never fails to return to the fundamental questions regarding student success.

And, for our Ya Yas and the Pink Ladies–they continue to remind us that it is always about people.

On a more personal note, we thank our parents—Sylvia Wallace, Don Wallace, Chris Webb, and Bob Webb. We list them individually because we are even more conscious now than ever of their individuality – their goals, their hopes, their paths, and their influence on us. We thank them for the full experience of life that they have given us and are aware that it is our responsibility not only to inherit and treasure this gift, but also to make it better and to pass it on.

To our husbands, Peter and Allen, and the Wallace Moseley boys, Mason and Walker. They listen to us, they laugh at and with us, and they love us and we are grateful. The process of student success has become even more personal as this work goes on. Mason is now in graduate school at Vanderbilt and Walker will graduate from NC State University this year, making "Learning and Your Life" our personal as well as our professional work.

Finally, to Appalachian students everywhere–you're the best. You are the reason we love going to work each day.

REFERENCE ACKNOWLEDGMENTS

We are particularly grateful to Katy R. Murphy who provided permission for us to use the ideas she presented at the First Year Experience Conference in a session called "Gaming: A Faculty Primer," Columbia, South Carolina, February, 1995.

Throughout this book, we have used the ideas, sample lectures, and handouts prepared by present and former colleagues at Appalachian State University, Boone, North Carolina, for use in their courses, previously US 1150 Freshman Seminar and now UCO 1200 First Year Seminar. When there has been a specific individual associated with a particular idea, we have indicated that information. This by no means assumes that the authors lay claim to the rest of the ideas as new and/or original offerings to the field of teaching. We believe that we have inherited these ideas through our work in the profession and intend to honor those who have come before us by including them in this book.

I

OUR TEACHING PHILOSOPHY

AND

THE RESEARCH BASIS FOR P.O.W.E.R. LEARNING

Our Teaching Philosophy

Cindy Wallace and Joni Petschauer

Appalachian State University

"Good students are made, not born," according to Bob Feldman, the author of this course text. This complements our philosophy of teaching. We have to work hard to become good instructors and make our classes successful; these things don't "just happen." In courses that promote student success, the quality of conversation among the students is paramount. It is Feldman's intention for *P.O.W.E.R. Learning* to promote a provocative dialogue between him and the student. Like many student success texts, this text can be used without the structure of a course or a faculty member.

Our goal with this Instructor's Resource Manual is to provide ways for you to become a part of the dialogue between the author and your students, thus enhancing the level to which your students become engaged in that conversation. Textbooks provide a rich source of information pertinent to a course's content. *P.O.W.E.R. Learning* will be a fundamental resource that will support your students in their journey to learn. A variety of alternative paths can be used to arrive at different levels of expertise. Just as there is no single path to becoming a good student, there is no single path to becoming a good instructor for this course. Teaching practices and activities that have worked for you in more traditional, content-specific courses, may or may not work for you here–just as one learning skill or strategy may work for one student and not another. Your learning philosophy is revealed by your assignment of specific chapters and exercises. As seasoned faculty, we take a textbook and use it to support and substantiate the lessons we believe are most important to teach.

At the heart of our instruction is the belief that we are building an academic community. We are sharing with students the rules of and reasons for being a part of that world. Thus, pervasive in our instruction is creating links between knowledge and action. We will be intentional in providing you with ways to use the course content that promotes an active demonstration of knowledge by your students.

Thus, you must be engaged with this text and your class. Consider the questions that arise from the reading; "wonder…" out loud; be excited about the possibilities; be intentional about your learning; be prepared to experiment, examine, share, reject, and embrace the process of learning and living just as you are asking your students to do.

A Word about How This Manual Is Organized

Learning can be messy. As the instructor, you will be expected to set the tone for discourse, facilitate the discovery of information, and provide the overall structure for the course. But, when genuine conversations begin, there is no real way to predict where they will end. Thus, it is important to have strategies that can provide an understanding of what "just happened" when your students walk out the door. Depending on your course goals, there will be several options for you to choose from for working with the material in each chapter. Specifically, we will seek out activities that promote *shared inquiry through individual reflection, collaborative discourse, and community responses.*

The Research Basis for *P.O.W.E.R. Learning*

Robert S. Feldman

University of Massachusetts—Amherst

and

Christopher Poirier

Stonehill College

Despite having the ability to do well academically, many college students are not successful students. ***P.O.W.E.R. Learning: Strategies for Success in College and Life*** introduces students to the P.O.W.E.R. Learning process, an approach to systematically completing tasks based on five steps: *P*repare, *O*rganize, *W*ork, *E*valuate, and *R*ethink. Each step in the process provides students with appropriate strategies, tactics, techniques, hints, and tips to will help them achieve academic success.

Is there a need for such an approach? Absolutely. For many first-year students, the demands of college are too great. Retention rates beyond the first year are often disappointing and sometimes dismal. Nationally, one-third of first-year students drop out after their first year, and in public community colleges, the dropout rate approaches 50 percent. Ultimately, only half of all students who start college complete it.

Many, if not most, of the students who fail to graduate from college do not leave because they are intellectually unable to do the work. Instead, they lack basic skills and knowledge of the strategies that lead to success in college, such as time management proficiency, effective writing abilities, understanding of how to read coursework effectively, skills in effective note taking, and knowledge of test taking strategies.

Yet these skills can be taught and taught in ways that lead to success. In fact, careful research finds that courses that teach the skills related to college success—known generically as "first-year experience courses" or FYE courses—produce a significant and demonstrable rise in student retention beyond the first semester in college. Furthermore, students who participate in FYE courses have higher grade point averages, are more satisfied with their college experience and institution, and have a stronger sense of community (Howard & Jones, 2000; Starke, Harth, & Sirianni, 2001; Schnell & Doetkott, 2003; Schnell, Louis, & Doetkott, 2003; Upcraft et al., 2004; Barefoot & Gardner, 2005; Feldman, 2005).

The P.O.W.E.R. Learning process seeks to maximize the success of students enrolled in first-year seminars by using a research-based "best practices" approach. It is the first scientifically-based approach to achieving first-year student success, with each step in the process based on sound, empirical research findings related to students' academic performance in a college environment. We will consider each of the five steps in the P.O.W.E.R. Learning process, discussing the scientific basis of each step.

Prepare

The first step in the P.O.W.E.R. Learning process is preparation. Before getting started on any task, preparation is necessary. The most critical facet of preparation is setting goals. Locke and Latham (1990) describe four reasons why goal setting improves performance. First, students who set goals direct their attention to the task they want to complete. Second, goals provide something to strive for which can motivate students. Third, students who set goals are less likely to be distracted. Finally, students who set goals are more likely than those who do not to use new strategies to reach their goals, especially when old strategies fail. These findings suggest that college students who possess effective goal-setting skills can improve their academic performance.

Research on goal setting also suggests that specific goals that are moderately difficult and attainable can enhance motivation and persistence (Pintrich & Schunk, 1996; Stipek, 1996). It is clear that students who set realistic, attainable goals are more likely to adjust successfully to college life than those who do not (Robbins & Schwitzer, 1988). In addition, academic performance is generally higher for students who set appropriate goals that meet their needs (Raterink, 2002). High-goal directed individuals, those who possess the ability to create appropriate goals, are often described as optimistic, persistent, and resourceful. On the other hand, low-goal directed individuals are generally pessimistic, reserved, unassuming, worried, and cautious (Payne, Robbins, & Dougherty, 1991; Robbins, Lese, & Herrick, 1993).

It is clear then that the goal-setting literature supports the view that goal setting is a necessary component for high performance. The P.O.W.E.R. Learning process includes goal setting so that students will be better prepared to set goals, and hence have something to strive toward. However, preparing for the future by setting goals is just the first step in the process of becoming a successful student.

Organize

The goals set during the preparation step cannot be accomplished without organization. First-year college students often need to adjust to busier schedules, multiple deadlines, and more difficult coursework in a short period of time. By staying organized, physically as well as intellectually, students will save time and be more likely to accomplish their goals (Swami, 1990; Dvorak, 1998). Organization of academic materials promotes better mastery and recall, especially if the material is difficult to understand (Woolfolk, 1998). Since many college courses are demanding and challenging, organized students have an advantage over unorganized students.

Whether students are writing a paper, preparing for a presentation, or taking notes, the organization of ideas and information is critical (Swami, 1990; Dvorak, Walz-Chojnacki, Staley, & Staley III, 1998). Not surprisingly, students prefer to be taught material that is clearly organized (Matthews, 1991). An organized class structure, which includes specific outlines, notes, assignments, and requirements, helps students to keep themselves organized. Moreover, students who use the organizational patterns in the material can help themselves in activities such as note taking (Stencel, 2001).

Another area of research shows that people with specialized knowledge in a particular field organize information to optimize learning (Schneider & Bjorklund, 1992; Anderson, 1993). In one study, soccer experts learned and remembered more new soccer terms than soccer novices. The soccer experts were able to mentally organize the new soccer terms enhancing their abilities to master the material (Schneider & Bjorklund, 1992). In short, the results of the expert knowledge studies and certain problem solving studies suggest that mental organization is a key to success. According to the research, college students benefit from being organized, and their organization leads to higher academic performance (Schneider & Bjorklund, 1992; Bransford & Stein, 1993).

Work

The third step in the P.O.W.E.R. Learning process is work. A student's level of motivation is a particularly important factor in determining success during this step (Covington, 2000; Robbins, Lauver, Le, Davis, Langley, & Carlstrom, 2004). Motivation is the force that guides people to strive for their goals.

One classic cognitive theory of motivation describes two types of motivation: intrinsic and extrinsic. Intrinsic motivation drives people to do something because it is rewarding on its own merits. People motivated intrinsically will strive to reach their goals because they find the work meaningful and interesting (Raffini, 1996; Reeve, 1996). Extrinsic motivation drives people to do things for a tangible reward, such as grades or money. Research suggests that people work harder and perform better when they are motivated intrinsically (Harackiewicz & Elliot, 1993; Elliot & Harackiewicz, 1996; Ryan & Deci, 1996; Lin, McKeachie, & Kim, 2001).

Closely related to research on motivation is research on how one's locus of control is related to college performance. Students tend to have primarily an internal or an external locus of control, and those with an internal locus of control tend to attribute their success to hard work (Kishor, 1983). On the other hand, students with an external locus of control attribute their success to luck, fate, or chance (Ashkanasy & Gallois, 1987). Often, students with an external locus of control will put little effort into their work since they do not believe their effort really matters. Not surprisingly, research has found that students with an internal locus of control earn higher grades than students with an external locus of control (Rose, Hall, Bolen, & Webster, 1996; Carden, Bryant, & Moss, 2004). Furthermore, locus of control is a good predictor of individual course and overall grade point average (Rose et al., 1996).

P.O.W.E.R Learning has been designed to improve students' motivation and, in particular, to help students to view success as a product of their hard work and effort. Research suggests that courses stressing study skills and adjustment skills can raise grade point averages and teach students to develop a greater internal locus of control (Cone & Owens, 1991).

Evaluate

Evaluate, the fourth step in the P.O.W.E.R. Learning process, leads students to compare their completed work with the goals they originally set. Students need to understand that completed work is not finished until they have evaluated it. All too often students do not recognize the importance of evaluating their work and often fail to revise their work, which can lead to lower performance. The literature on writing, for example, clearly shows that first-year college students need to revise their writing in order to meet their goals and to achieve good grades (Flower, Hayes, Carey, Schriver, & Stratman, 1986; Hill, Wallace, & Haas, 1992).

Recent research indicates that it is possible to teach inexperienced writers how to revise their work successfully (Wallace et al., 1996; Cook, 2001; Harris, 2003; Sloane, 2003). In one study, for example, students wrote essays, received and gave peer reviews, received instructors' reviews, and then revised their essays. Students involved in this process showed improved writing skills, which caused them to write better essays (Athhauser & Darnall, 2001).

Building on this literature, *P.O.W.E.R. Learning* provides students with the necessary instruction and tips for how to evaluate their work. According to the research mentioned above, these instructions and tips can improve students' performance and promote academic success.

Rethink

The fifth step in the P.O.W.E.R Learning process—rethink—consists of bringing a fresh eye to what has already been accomplished. In contrast to evaluation, which involves considering whether the initial goals have been achieved, rethinking consists of a reconsideration of the process that has been used to achieve the goals.

Rethinking requires the use of *critical thinking*, thinking that involves analyzing, questioning, and challenging underlying assumptions. Critical thinking is "purposeful, reasoned, and goal-directed" (Halpern, 1998), and it involves higher order cognitive skills that students need to possess. People use critical thinking to solve problems, formulate hypotheses, make decisions, and evaluate outcomes. With the increasing advances in technology, science, and other fields, college students need to possess critical-thinking skills. Students who can think critically will be better prepared for college and for careers after college. This is one important reason why it is important to introduce critical thinking at the beginning of students' college careers (Halpern, 1998; 2003).

Research suggests that students can become better critical thinkers if they are given the proper instruction and are exposed to a curriculum that stresses critical thinking. Researchers found that students involved in critical thinking and problem-solving exercises scored higher on a critical-thinking inventory than students who were not involved in the exercises (Perkins, Jay, & Tishman, 1993; Reed & Kromrey, 2001; Halpern, 2003; Burbach, Matkin, & Fritz, 2004). Gadzella, Ginther, & Bryant (1997) found critical thinking skills to be the best predictor of course grades in an introductory psychology course. Students who earned A's in the course had higher critical-thinking scores than students who earned C's in the same course. In a more recent study (Williams, Oliver, Allin, Winn, & Booher, 2003), students' critical-thinking skills predicted exam grades in a human development course. Although the results are correlational, they show a strong relationship between critical-thinking skills and grades that should not be overlooked.

The literature thus suggests that a student's ability to rethink and reanalyze their work is just as important as setting goals and following through with the work. Students who use critical thinking skills can achieve higher grades, solve more difficult problems, and make better decisions.

Conclusion

It is clear that each of the steps embodied in the P.O.W.E.R. Learning process—which forms the basis for *P.O.W.E.R. Learning: Strategies for Success in College and Life*—has a firm foundation in the research literature. By using the steps outlined in the P.O.W.E.R. Learning process, students will be able to maximize their opportunities for success, both in and out of the classroom.

References

Althauser, R., & Darnall, K. (2001). Enhancing critical reading and writing through peer reviews: An exploration of assisted performance. *Teaching Sociology, 29*, 23-35.

Anderson, J. R. (1993). Problem solving and learning. *American Psychologist, 48*, 35-44.

Ashkanasy, N. M., & Gallois, C. (1987). Locus of control and attributions for academic performance of self and others. *Australian Journal of Psychology, 39*, 293-305.

Bransford, J. D., & Stein, B. S. (1993). *The IDEAL problem solver: A guide for improving thinking learning, and creativity* (2nd ed.). New York: Freemen.

Barefoot, B.O, & Gardner, J.N. (Eds.) (2005). Achieving and sustaining institutional excellence for the first year of college. San Francisco: Jossey-Bass.

Burbach, M. E., Matkin, G. S., & Fritz, S. M. (2004). Teaching critical thinking in an introductory leadership course utilizing active learning strategies: A confirmatory study. *College Student Journal, 38*, 482-493.

Busby, R. R., Gammel, H. L., & Jeffcoat, N. K. (2002). Grades, graduation, and orientation: A longitudinal study of how new student programs relate to grade point average and graduation. *Journal of College Orientation and Transition, 10*, 45-57.

Carden, R., Bryant, C., & Moss, R. (2004). Locus of control, text anxiety, academic procrastination, and achievement among college students. *Psychological Reports, 95*, 581-582.

Cone, A. L. & Owens, S. K. (1991). Academic and locus of control enhancement in a freshmen study skills and college adjustment course. *Psychological Reports, 68*, 1211-1217.

Cook, D. (2001). Revising editing. *Teaching English in the Two-Year College, 29*, 154-161.

Covington, M. V. (2000). Goal theory, motivation, and school achievement: An integrative review. *Annual Review of Psychology, 51*, 171-200.

Dvorak, J. (1998). Time management: The foundation of academic success. In J.N Gardner & A.J. Jewler (Eds.), *Your college experience: Strategies for success* (pp. 39-58). Belmont, CA: Wadsworth.

Dvorak J., Walz-Chojnacki, M., Staley, C. C., Staley III, R. S. (1998). Making the grade: Taking exams and giving speeches. In J. N Gardner & A. J. Jewler (Eds.), *Your college experience: Strategies for success* (pp.113-138). Belmont, CA: Wadsworth.

Elliot, A. J., & Harackiewicz, J. M. (1996). Approach and avoidance achievement goals and intrinsic motivation: A mediational analysis. *Journal of Personality and Social Psychology, 70*, 461-475.

Feldman, R.S. (Ed.) (2005). *Improving the First Year of College: Research and Practice.* Mahwah, NJ: Erlbaum.

Flower, L., Hayes, J. R., Carey, L., Schriver, K., & Stratman, J. (1986). Detection, diagnosis, and the strategies of revision. *College Composition and Communication, 37*, 16-55.

Gadzella, B. M., Ginther, D. W., & Bryant, G. W. (1997). Prediction of performance in an academic course by scores on measures of learning style and critical thinking. *Psychological Reports, 81*, 595-602.

Halpern, D. F. (1998). Teaching critical thinking for transfer across domains. *American Psychologist, 53*, 449-455.

Halpern, D. F. (2003). *Thought & knowledge: An introduction to critical thinking* (4th ed.). Mahwah, NJ: Lawrence Erlbaum Associates.

Harackiewicz, J. M., & Elliot, A. J. (1993). Achievement goals and intrinsic motivation. *Journal of Personality and Social Psychology, 65*, 904-915.

Harris, J. (2003). Revision as a critical practice. *College English, 65*, 577-592.

Hill, C., Wallace, D. L., & Haas, C. (1992). Revising on-line: Computer technologies and the revision process. *Computers and Composition, 9*, 83-109.

Howard, H. E., & Jones, W. P. (2000). Effectiveness of a freshman seminar in an urban university: Measurement of selected indicators. *College Student Journal, 34*, 509-515.

Kishor, N. (1983). Locus of control and academic achievement. *Journal of Cross-Cultural Psychology, 14*, 297-308.

Lin, Y., McKeachie, W. J., & Kim, Y. C. (2001). College student intrinsic and/or extrinsic motivation and learning. *Learning & Individual Differences, 13*, 251-258.

Locke, E A., & Latham, G. P. (1990). *A theory of goal setting and task performance.* Englewood Cliffs, NJ: Prentice-Hall.

Matthews, D. B. (1991). Learning styles research: Implications for increasing students in teacher education programs. *Journal of Instructional Psychology, 18*, 228-236.

Payne, E. C., Robbins, S. B., & Dougherty, L. (1991). Goal directedness and older adult adjustment. *Journal of Counseling Psychology, 38*, 300-308.

Perkins, D., Jay, E., & Tishman, S. (1993). New conceptions of thinking: From ontology to education. *Educational psychologist, 28*, 67-85.

Pintrich, P. R., & Schunk, D. H. (1996). *Motivation in education: Theory, research, and applications.* Columbus, OH: Merrill.

Raffini, J. P. (1996). *150 ways to increase intrinsic motivation in the classroom.* Boston: Allyn & Bacon.

Raterink, G. V. (2002). Why do some students succeed? *American School Board Journal, 189*(2), 31.

Reed, J. H., & Kromrey, J. D. (2001). Teaching critical thinking in a community college history course: Empirical evidence from infusing Paul's model. *College Student Journal, 35*, 201-215.

Reeve, J. (1996). *Motivating others: Nurturing inner motivational resources.* Boston: Allyn & Bacon.

Robbins, S. B., Lauver, K., Le, H., Davis, D., Langley, R., & Carlstrom, A. (2004). Do psychosocial and study skill factors predict college outcomes? A meta-analysis. *Psychological Bulletin, 130*, 261-288.

Robbins, S. B., Lese, K. P., & Herrick, S. M. (1993). Interactions between goal instability and social support on college freshman adjustment. *Journal of Counseling and Development, 71*, 343-348.

Robbins, S., & Schwitzer, A. (1988). A validity study of the Superiority and Goal Instability Scales as predictors of women's adjustment to college life. *Measurement and Evaluation in Counseling and Development, 21*, 117-123.

Rose, R. J., Hall, C. W., Bolen, L. M., & Webster, R. E. (1996). Locus of control and college students approaches to learning. *Psychological Reports, 79*, 163-171.

Ryan, R. M., & Deci, E. L. (1996). When paradigms clash: Comments on Cameron and Pierce's claim that rewards do not undermine intrinsic motivation. *Review of Educational Research, 66*, 33-38.

Schneider, W., & Bjorklund, D. F. (1992). Expertise, aptitude, and strategic remembering. *Child Development, 63*, 416-473.

Schnell, C. A., & Doetkott, C. D. (2003). First year seminars produce long-term impact. *Journal of College Student Retention, 4*, 377-391.

Schnell, C. A., Louis, K. S., & Doetkott, C. (2003). The first-year seminar as a means of improving college graduation rates. *Journal of the First-Year Experience & Students in Transition, 15*(1), 53-75.

Sloane, B. S. (2003). Say it straight: Teaching conciseness. *Teaching English in the Two-Year College, 30*, 429-433.

Starke, M. C., Harth, M., & Sirianni, F. (2001). Retention, bonding, and academic achievement: Success of a first-year seminar. *Journal of the First-Year Experience & Students in Transition, 13*(2), 7-35.

Stencel, J. E. (2001). Note-taking techniques in the science classroom: Focusing on the important concepts in science. *Journal of College Science Teaching, 30*, 403-405.

Stipek, D. J. (1996). Motivation and Instruction. In D. Berliner & R. Calfee (Eds.), *Handbook of educational psychology* (pp.85-109). New York: Macmillan.

Strahan, E. Y. (2003). The effects of social anxiety and social skills on academic performance. *Personality and Individual Differences, 34*, 347-366.

Swami, S. A. (1990). *The college student's handbook for better grades, job search, and career success.* Montgomery, WV: Minibook.

Upcraft, M. L., Gardner, J. N., & Barefoot, B.O., & Associates. (2004). *Challenging and supporting the first-year student: A handbook for improving the first year of college.* San Francisco: Jossey-Bass.

Wallace, D. L., Hayes, J. R., Hatch, J. A., Moller, W., Moser, G., & Silk, C. M. (1996). Better revision in eight minutes? Prompting first-year college students to revise globally. *Journal of Educational Psychology, 88*, 682-688.

Williams, R. L., Oliver, R., Allin, J. L., Winn, B., & Booher, C. S. (2003). Psychological critical thinking as a course predictor and outcome variable. *Teaching of Psychology, 30*, 220-223.Woolfolk, A. E. (1998). *Educational psychology*. Boston: Allyn & Bacon.

II

COURSE DEVELOPMENT AND CLASSROOM

MANAGEMENT TIPS

INTRODUCTION

From the heading of this section, it is obvious that this is a nuts-and-bolts approach—the "how to" of a student success course. Although Appalachian State University serves as the model, we believe this information about course development and classroom management tips can be applied to any academic success course at any university, college or community college.

Included in this section, you will find:

- Goals for Freshman Seminar

- Course Content Recommendations

- Syllabi Examples

- Engaging Students–Promising Practices

- Student Assessment

- Course Evaluation

There are many solid first-year experience programs at universities and colleges throughout the United States and the world. We encourage you to learn about the efforts being made to support first-year students and to create a model that has meaning and application on your own campus. We have found the individuals who are advocates for this work to be generous with their time and materials. Don't hesitate to call on colleagues from other schools as you develop your program. Let these ideas serve as a foundation for your own solutions.

GOALS FOR FRESHMAN SEMINAR

The goal of a seminar course is to establish new relationships, to build academic and life skills, to provide opportunities for personal growth and the broadening of perspectives, and to understand what it means to be an educated person.

Develop intellectual and academic competence
- Students will continue to develop their abilities in critical thinking, writing, reading, communicating, and problem solving.
- Students will strengthen study skills, including note taking and test taking.
- Students will understand their own learning styles.
- Students will appreciate what it means to be an educated person and understand the value of a college degree.
- Students will develop effective introductory academic computing skills.
- Students will understand how to effectively utilize the library and how to locate and evaluate electronic information.

Establish and maintain interpersonal relationships (build community)
- Students will develop connections with students, faculty, advisors, and the university community that support and enrich a successful college experience.

Manage transition
- Students will learn strategies to manage stress.
- Students will discuss issues related to alcohol and drug awareness, with the aspiration to make mature and healthy decisions.
- Students will develop and practice effective time-management strategies.

Broaden horizons and personal development
- Students will be exposed to cultural opportunities.
- Students will gain an awareness and appreciation for multiculturalism and diversity.
- Students will be provided a structured opportunity to reflect on who they are, what they value, and what they want out of life.
- Students will seek clarity about career goals and will be introduced to campus resources, such as Peer Career and Career Development Center that will help them in the career exploration process.

Discover your university
- Students will learn about campus resources that could enrich and support their educational experience.
- Students will learn about campus policies and regulations, including the code of academic conduct, safety responsibilities and protocols, registration information, and general education requirements.
- Students will learn about the history and traditions of your university and its region.
- Students will understand the importance of getting involved in co-curricular activities and how to pursue these opportunities.

COMMON COURSE REQUIREMENTS

Introduction

Freshman Seminar offers first semester students a carefully structured orientation to college, an introduction to academic and personal success strategies, and an opportunity for self-discovery and self-realization. It draws on national models and extensive research for much of its conceptual framework, but is tailored to fit the unique needs and challenges faced by your campus. The following is an example of a set of common course requirements that may serve as a guide for your institution.

I. Course Management

A. Syllabus

Your course syllabus sets a tone for class. It shows your planning and commitment, your expectations and concerns, your goals and enthusiasm for the semester. The syllabus is your public statement of purpose, which students will rely on throughout the semester. University policy requires that every student in your class receive a syllabus on the first day of class. You are also required to keep a copy of your syllabus on file in the Freshman Seminar office. Please submit a copy of your syllabus by the opening of the term. University regulations and standard practice also specify a number of required components to your syllabus. These include:

- **general information** about the course (the title, course number, meeting place and time, and semester, contact info, campus address, phone number, and e-mail address)
- **statement of your purposes/goals/objectives** in teaching the course
- **enumeration of course requirements and goals**; our central purpose in Freshman Seminar is to help entering students be successful. This involves support in a wide range of areas from establishing new relationships and building academic and life skills to providing opportunities for personal growth and broadening of personal perspectives. A more complete statement of program goals is contained in the training manual. Be certain to keep these goals in mind as you work out your course requirements.
- **list of required readings**; give a complete bibliographic citation and tell students that the book can be obtained as a "rental text" at the University bookstore. Reference any additional required readings and associated costs. See Section D below for more information about readings in Freshman Seminar.
- **list of office hours** (regular hours and other times available for student conferences); we recommend that you be available on campus for Freshman Seminar students for two to three hours per week.
- **attendance policy**; attendance policies should be designed to encourage participation rather than penalize students. Freshman Seminar usually requires out-of-class attendance at events such as the Group Interaction Course (GIC), cultural events, and dinner at the faculty member's home. Freshman Seminar encourages instructors to be flexible with students who have schedule conflicts and to reassign a set time for out-of-class events where appropriate. The University requires that you spell out your attendance policy in your syllabus.
- **your grading policy (Freshman Seminar is a letter-graded course)**; you must make qualitative assessments of all submitted student work. We do not expect that all our students will receive A's. Please do not grade Freshman Seminar as a pass/fail course. We do not wish to focus or reward mere quantitative completion of assignment, attendance, and

participation. It is very important that you make *qualitative* assessments with appropriate feedback on each student's work. It is also very important that this course have high academic standards comparable to other first-year courses. You should clearly spell out your grading. Students expect to know how they will be graded and require that we explain our grading policy in our syllabus.

- **class outline**; you do not need to have all class activities predetermined and listed in the syllabus. In fact, it is probably better not to do so. Stay flexible so that you may respond to the needs of your students. Student and class personas vary. List assignments in whatever detail you deem appropriate. However, we urge you to include institutional calendar dates that will affect your course, such as the last date to drop a course, convocation, holidays, last day of classes, etc. Remember to specify examination dates, GIC date if available, Open House, and other special dates in your course. We advise you to look at sample syllabi, which are on file in the Freshman Seminar office.

B. Class Budget

One unique advantage we enjoy when teaching Freshman Seminar is our class budget. Academic Affairs supplies each class with $15 per student to pay for the GIC ($5), cultural activities ($5), and feeding students at your home or in the class setting ($5). The purpose of this money is to support community building within your class, stronger faculty-student connections, and a friendlier atmosphere in your class. The Freshman Seminar office will assist you in scheduling and paying for the GIC, and we will also purchase and deliver cultural events tickets to you. Itemized receipts for food purchases or other expenditures within your $15/student limit must be turned in to the Freshman Seminar office for reimbursement.

C. Course Evaluation

Institutional policy requires that all classes be evaluated once a year. Freshman Seminar students participate in a standard course and instructor evaluation at the end of the semester. The Freshman Seminar office provides evaluation forms. Student evaluation results are returned to instructors early the following semester. A copy of the current evaluation form is in the Faculty Training Manual. In addition to the end of course evaluations, students will complete the online version of the First-Year Initiative Survey (FYI) sponsored by the Policy Center on the First Year of College. We encourage you to conduct a *midterm evaluation* and seek regular student feedback throughout the semester. Students buy into a course in which they feel a sense of ownership.

D. Required Readings

1. Textbook. Freshman Seminar has always utilized a textbook to achieve common course content. The textbook selection committee designed a custom edition of Robert Feldman's *P.O.W.E.R. Learning*, coupled with numerous articles, as our new common text. This textbook and its supporting materials provide a valuable framework for Freshman Seminar classes.
2. *New Connections: A Freshman Seminar Handbook*. In its fourth edition, this campus specific handbook provides a compendium of information used in Freshman Seminar classes, segments on computing, institutional history, Myers-Briggs, campus resources, money management, wellness, and other topics provide a convenient and essential resource for

students. All Freshman Seminar classes use *New Connections,* which is available for purchase through the bookstore.

3. Supplementary Reading. Freshman Seminar is a college class. We believe that there is not enough required reading during the undergraduate years, especially in the first year. With this in mind, Freshman Seminar students should read at least one, but no more than two, supplementary books or novels. We think that the assignment of major collateral reading relevant to the first year experience is essential for better reading habits and to demonstrate more effective reading strategies. Many instructors have used popular novels like *Iron and Silk* by Mark Salzman or *The Kite Runner* by Khalid Hosseini. Novels about people at a transition point in life have been particularly effective. Instructors may also want to consider *Freakonomics* by Stephen Dubner and Steven Levitt, the summer reading book for this year's students. It will be distributed to all first year students during orientation. Instructors may pick up a free desk copy from the bookstore. Numerous additional possibilities are listed in the training manual and on the Freshman Seminar Home Page: www.freshmanseminar.appstate.edu.

Readings should be discussed thoroughly and incorporated into class discourse. They can be the subjects for writing assignments and class examinations. Encouraging reading for pleasure and information, for self-fulfillment and personal development can be one of the most powerful contributions we make in Freshman Seminar.

II. Building Community

A. Group Interaction Course (GIC)

One of the most popular required activities in Freshman Seminar is the Group Interaction Course. Students report that it is a powerful experience. They tell us that its impact reaches far beyond the group challenges, class fun, and individual self-discovery that occurs. It raises them to a new level of understanding about what college means. All of this happens outside the classroom, away from campus, in the quiet beauty of the University Woods. The GIC becomes a metaphor for building community, valuing difference, seeking instruction, planning, dealing with criticism and failure, focusing attention, managing time, and many other things related to college success. Because it has proven to be such a valuable student experience, we have agreed that *all classes will participate in the GIC* early in the semester, preferably in September. Contact the Freshman Seminar office to sign up for a time. (Consult the faculty-training manual for additional information about preparation, participation, and follow-up class assignments.)

B. Service Project

Last year over half of all Freshman Seminar classes engaged in some form of service project. A service project can advance class goals, especially community building and discovering our campus. Furthermore, service projects can strengthen helping, communication, and coping skills. They can broaden perspectives, develop human-interaction skills, and teach first year students how to handle new kinds of responsibility. Service learning can help students identify and define future student and life roles. If you decide to undertake a service project, our experience shows that these work best when performed as a whole class. We encourage you to consider a service project.

III. Strengthening Learning Skills

A. Learning Skills

Students reported last fall that they would have to improve their learning skills to succeed in college. Anecdotal evidence suggests that many first year students continue to use the same approaches ("tools") that worked in high school—even though they do not always work in college. With this in mind, we must address learning skills more directly in Freshman Seminar if we are to prepare students to be successful in their majors and beyond. Consequently, each class must introduce note taking skills, test taking strategies, and college reading strategies. Our new textbook, faculty resource manual, and resource room offer numerous useable approaches. Learning-skills activities should be woven together throughout the semester with other course objectives. Practicing note taking during a lecture on campus history offers one possibility: consider introducing new reading strategies while studying collateral reading (perhaps the text from the linked course). Strengthening learning skills equips students with more and better "tools" for success in college.

B. Use of the Library

Students must learn how to use the library and information commons if they want to succeed in college. Students will benefit throughout their college and professional lives from this initial introduction. It can best be accomplished by integrating a library research component into at least one class assignment. Every student could complete this online library tutorial quiz. Second, library staff will work with instructors to develop relevant assignments requiring use of library resources. Finally, library personnel should introduce students to resources available in the Electronic Library Classroom and then support their individual research efforts. The goal is to show first year students how to make use of modern library resources for both general information and discipline specific purposes. At a minimum, students will learn how to locate books, journal articles, reference materials, and use electronic databases. Every class must participate in a library visit that includes a session in the Electronic Library Classroom. To prepare for this assignment, schedule a class visit, or find out more about this component call the Library Resource Office.

IV. Managing Transition

A. Time Management

Up to this point, school, family, and work have determined the lives of our first year students overwhelmingly. Now we ask them to manage 168 hours each college week in a largely unstructured environment. This can be challenging for first year students. Accordingly, each Freshman Seminar class must address effective strategies in time management.

B. Wellness

First Year students often overlook the importance of wellness in their success strategies. Experience shows that students who do not employ proper wellness strategies often get derailed during their first semester. Freshman Seminar must confront wellness issues beyond Open House visits to the infirmary. Stress, personal health, sexually transmitted diseases, and responsible alcohol and drug decision making, as well as personal safety must be addressed. This can be accomplished by developing individual approaches drawn from faculty training, utilizing suggestions in the Faculty Resource Manual, or calling on professionals in the Health Center or Counseling Center. We cannot ignore or downplay the importance of these topics in student success.

C. Money Management

Learning to manage money is one of the most difficult challenges new college students face. Even though our students may be receiving money from home, they may never have had to manage their finances before. Living on a limited budget, avoiding the lure of credit cards, and establishing a good credit history are new challenges for students. Decisions made now may strongly affect their financial future. This is the time in their life to start learning smart money management. Freshman Seminar should address the important issues of budgeting and establishing good credit.

V. Discovering Our Campus

A. Walk for Awareness

Freshman Seminar classes are encouraged to attend the Walk for Awareness. This annual event, held on the Tuesday after Labor Day, provides a powerful forum to discuss campus and personal safety.

B. Convocation

Freshman Seminar classes participate in fall convocation. Experience has shown that we need to prepare students ahead of time with information about the speaker and the topic. A writing assignment connected to convocation and the summer reading book adds interest and enthusiasm to the event. Attending as a class can help to build community outside the classroom. Follow up discussions can address important common issues confronting our entire academic community.

C. Open House

Each fall the Freshman Seminar Office organizes an Open House designed to introduce students to support services and personnel that may be critical to their success. Classes visit the Learning Assistance Program, Health Services, Peer Career Office, and Counseling Center. Visits are scheduled in the late afternoon or early evening and usually last about one hour and twenty minutes. Instructors are expected to attend with their classes. Many instructors substitute Open House for one class period. Most connect an assignment or quiz to this activity to ensure student accountability. Dates for this year's Open House are being finalized. More information will be forthcoming shortly. Each class is expected to participate in this informational program.

D. Campus Involvement

National studies show that students succeed at higher rates when they are actively involved in campus life. Involvement can, of course, be carried too far, leaving no time for academic or personal life. But modest involvement can make an important difference. As a result, Freshman Seminar instructors have long felt that each first year student must become involved in one campus organization of their choice during their first semester. There is a wide range of options, including official clubs, intramural sports, religious activities, or perhaps even employment. Selection should be preceded by a discussion of what constitutes a campus organization, criteria for involvement, pros and cons of involvement, and the overall benefits of membership or participation.

E. Campus History

Freshman Seminar offers the only class that introduces first year students to the past of our campus. Our history presents a unique vehicle for discovering identity and understanding our purpose. A minimum of one class must be spent on the history of our campus. Talking about history usually comes later in the semester, after other more basic things like community building, transitions, and learning skills have been introduced. Some instructors have scheduled the history session around homecoming to add substance, flavor, and context to a student's early college experience.

VI. Broadening Horizons

A. Myers-Briggs

The Myers-Briggs Type Inventory is the most widely used personality assessment instrument in the world. It is not a diagnostic tool for psychological problems or a scale of positive or negative behaviors. It helps us understand human differences and our preferred styles of learning and behavior. We employ the MBTI to help students meet the challenges of the classroom and campus. It can be a very powerful teaching and motivational tool with first year students and can be connected with learning skills, diversity issues, understanding professors, roommate problems, relationship issues, career exploration, and a host of other Freshman Seminar topics. Resource persons will be available fall semester to present this concept to your class. In order to maximize time, we ask that classes pair up for the presentations. A minimum of one full class is needed to explain and demonstrate the concepts. Assignments utilizing MBTI can be integrated into other topics throughout the semester.

B. Cultural Events

Astronomy Professor Daniel Caton once wrote that "going to college and only attending the popular music events would be like flying to France for vacation and eating only at McDonald's." Cultural experiences are an important part of a liberal arts education. They broaden horizons, open new worlds, and offer opportunities for self-discovery and expression. Freshman Seminar students are expected to attend at least one University-sponsored cultural event. A portion of our class budget supports ticket purchases for cultural events. Integrate the event you or your class chooses into your class themes. Explain to students that we value cultural events because they build community, broaden horizons, expand our appreciation of diversity, help us discover more about our institution, and enhance our understanding of what a liberal arts education means. Attending a cultural event is also an opportune time to organize a meal with our class.

C. Learning Communities Involvement

The most important new academic initiative of the past decade is our Freshman Learning Communities (FLC) initiative. These link each Freshman Seminar class with one other academic class, sometimes English or history. Students are co-enrolled in both classes, class activities are coordinated, and instructors meet periodically to talk about the students with an academic advisor. The results have been remarkable. Students are more successful and feel more connected, supported, and engaged. Faculty learns to share and interact in new academic ways. And students have the benefit of a three-person support team (Freshman Seminar instructor, instructor in the other academic class, and an academic advisor) working to support their success. We urge you to participate fully and enthusiastically in your Learning Community. They expand our Freshman Seminar community in valuable ways.

D. Majors and Career Planning

Retention research has clearly demonstrated a correlation between career development and graduation. A clearly thought out career path can provide the focus, motivation, and determination needed to persevere to graduation. Therefore, it is important that each class of Freshman Seminar address major and career development issues, probably in the second half of the semester. This can be done with textbook or Web-based assignments, by visiting the Peer-Career office, or by inviting individuals from the Career Development Center to your class. Academic advisors are also equipped to facilitate this component in connection with developing a four-year plan and choosing a major. The career component of your course should result in three activities:

1. introduction to online career resources, including the Career Development Center's Website and the online *Occupation Outlook Handbook*
2. visit to the Peer Career Office to explore majors and careers
3. discussion of or development of a professional resume

E. International Programs

Understanding our world is more important today than ever before. Global events and trends shape our work, votes, and future more than ever seemed possible a generation ago. We can learn about our global society in the classroom, but a more powerful and increasingly viable way of discovering our world is to study abroad. Representatives from International Programs can arrange group presentations to explain study abroad opportunities to our students.

F. Appreciating Diversity

If we are to begin preparing students for an increasingly diverse world, we must address this issue in Freshman Seminar. Appreciating human diversity, whether it is racial, ethnic, gender, national, or physical is part of becoming an educated person today. Freshman Seminar supports this goal wholeheartedly and each class should explore issues of diversity.

G. Academic Integrity and Professional Ethics

Professional ethics and integrity are becoming more and more important in today's complex world. Expectations are rising with each revelation of poor judgment, illegal behavior, or questionable practice. As the first step toward preparing young professionals, each Freshman Seminar class will discuss our institution's academic integrity code, including its implications for today and tomorrow.

H. Liberal Arts Education

From our experience, first year students know very little about what it means to be a liberally educated person. They enter college without clearly understanding the goals of higher education. Freshman Seminar helps students understand the goals of a liberal arts education, the importance of academic integrity, the rituals and celebrations of the academic world (convocation), and the personal process of goal setting. We urge you to assign the article in *New Connections* on the liberal arts and to discuss this concept with your students.

SYLLABI EXAMPLES

Each section of Freshman Seminar reflects the individuality of the faculty member who teaches. We have included several examples of course syllabi from a variety of sources, including copies from our own most recent experiences teaching this course.

FRESHMAN SEMINAR US 1150
TUESDAY/THURSDAY   9:30–10:45 A.M.
SEMINAR SYLLABUS

This Freshman Seminar class is part of a Freshman Learning Community and is linked with HIS 110 (World Civilizations) taught by Dr. Rennie Brantz, brantzrw@appstate.edu on MWF 11:00–11:50, 103 Whitener Hall.

Your academic advisor is:

FRESHMAN SEMINAR INSTRUCTOR AND PEER LEADER

Cindy Wallace	Josh Ammons
109 B.B. Dougherty	PO Box XXXX
262-2060	peer leader phone number
wallaceca@appstate.edu	peerleaderemail@appstate.edu
Home: XXXX (before 9 P.M. please)	

REQUIRED TEXTS: Advising Planner 2008-2009
P.O.W.E.R. Learning, Robert Feldman
New Connections
Academic Planner (student calendar)
Freakonomics, by Stephen Dubner and Steven Levitt
New York Times

I. Seminar Purpose and Thoughts

The Freshman Seminar is a course designed especially for first year students—individuals like each of you who are entering higher education for the first time. The basic goal of the course is to help you cope successfully with the demands of college and to make the best use possible of the challenges and opportunities with which you will be confronted. It is our hope that you, through the course of the semester, will gain a better understanding of yourself, your fellow students, your instructors, and the University community. Most of all, we hope this course will stimulate your desire to learn during your years at Appalachian and the years beyond. As a member of a Freshman Learning Community, you have a unique opportunity to develop strong relationships with fellow students and with faculty. It is our hope that the partnership of these classes will help extend important academic discussions beyond our classroom and help you develop into a skilled collaborative learner.

II. Course Requirements/Expectations

Attendance: You are required to attend all class meetings. We will have regular class meetings beyond our scheduled class time. The success of the class depends on it. **Each student will be allowed only three absences.** Your grade will be lowered for each absence over the limit. We expect to be notified if you cannot attend. Any emergency absences should be explained to us as soon as possible. **Academic Integrity: I will follow Appalachian's Academic Integrity Policy in this course. Please read this policy. It is very important.**

III. Grading

This course will be graded on a letter grade basis. Your grade will be determined by participation, attendance, and your written work on required papers, exams, quizzes, and a presentation. The grading will be divided into four (not necessarily equal) parts:

> PART I. **Participation and attendance:** We will have approximately 30 meetings of this class; some meetings will be scheduled outside of our Tuesday/Thursday routine. You are expected to be in class, to be prepared, and to participate.

> PART II. **Quizzes, presentations, papers, admit cards:** At different times during the semester, we will assign papers based on topics discussed in class or on cultural programs we attend. We will also have a few quizzes or exams during the semester on class readings, speakers, or lectures. All written work should be kept in a binder that will be submitted at certain times during the semester and at the end of the semester as an academic portfolio review of your entire semester. You should have this binder with you in class everyday. All work—notes, admit cards, in class exercises, homework and out of class assignments—must be included. Admit cards, submitted as an e-mail, are due each Thursday. This e-mail should address the prompt specified in class by Cindy or Josh.

> PART III. **Presentation and paper:** Our learning community will have a shared assignment based on modernization that includes a research project, which culminates in a group presentation and a paper. You will be evaluated and receive credit in US 1150 and HIS 1102. We will also share the *New York Times* project as part of our learning community.

> PART IV. **The final project:** You will be asked to present a final project at the end of the semester. To this end, I want you to use the three-ring binder to keep all assignments (especially weekly admit cards and *New York Times* articles) and to create your Freshman Seminar portfolio. This project will be discussed throughout the semester.

IV. Reading Assignments: Assignments will be made from your text and other sources, as they are appropriate.

V. Course Topics and Outline: We want this course to be flexible enough to include both the topics we feel are important for your success at Appalachian and topics you feel a need to discuss. We would like your input and your help in planning the semester. The following topics are possibilities:

Section I. From High School to Appalachian: An Introduction to the Learning Community
- your living environment–residence hall life versus home life
- the University—what is it? What should it be?
- the University—background and history of Appalachian
- professors—who are they? Where do they come from?
- expectations and obligations
- academic regulations
- academic program planning

Section II. Understanding Appalachian: Surviving at Appalachian
- academic skills—note taking, test taking, study habits, computer skills
- time management
- cultural activities
- campus/community entertainment, involvement
- student organizations and activities
- assertiveness
- wellness
- creativity
- campus resources

Section III. Exploring Interests and Values
- discovery of self
- values clarification
- goals, dreams, service
- majors–career and majors
- becoming a lifelong learner, a world citizen
- tour and speakers, scheduled at your request

A detailed calendar for the class will be formulated by our joint effort during the second week of class and distributed to each student.

Several dates you should put on your calendar **NOW**:		
Convocation	Sept. 8	10:00 A.M. (no classes until 12:30, Assessment Day)
Walk for Awareness	Sept. 6	9:00 P.M.
Open House	Sept. 20	5:50-7:00 P.M.
GIC	Sept. 13	4:30-7:50 P.M.
Service Project	TBA	TBA

FRESHMAN SEMINAR
SCHEDULE OF ACTIVITIES

AUG	**23**	Introduction to course and to each other
	25	Name cards/schedule/goals for class
		Assignment: Chapter 1
	30	MBTI/Chapter 1
		Assignment: Reading 2 – R3 – R7 Journal
SEPT	**1**	On Becoming a Better Student
		Assignment: New Connections
	6	**Walk for Awareness** (meet 8:45 p.m. in front of D.D. Dougherty)
		Study groups – First LC quiz Sept. 9
	8	**Convocation** (meet 9:45 a.m. NW entrance Holmes Center)
	13	**No class at 9:30**
		GIC at 4:30 p.m. (meet at Outdoor Programs/Broome-Kirk Gym)
	15	MBTI/time management/note taking
		Assignment: Chapters 2, 4, *Power Learning*
	20	**No class at 9:30**
		Open House 4:50 p.m./D. D. Dougherty
	22	Research project introduction–library visit
	29	Chapter 5 Power Learning/Preparation for history exam
OCT	**4**	First assignment due–Chapter 6 *Power Learning & New York Times*
		Advisor visit & planner
	6	**Majors Fair 11–2 pm, Grandfather Mtn. Ballroom, Student Union**
	11	**Fall Break**
	13	Mid-term assessment
	18	International education/campus and community involvement
	20	Capitol steps?
	25	**Homecoming Weekend**–Appalachian history & traditions
	27	Freshman play? Movie night?
NOV	**1**	Chapter 7 *Power Learning*
		Reading 24, R-97-99
	3	Chapter 8 *Power Learning*
	8	Wellness/personal money management
	10	(ASU vs. Lees-McRae women's basketball opener)
	15	Presentations
	17	Presentations
	22	Presentations
	24	**Happy Thanksgiving**
	29	Exam preparation
DEC	**1**	Review/evaluation/advisor visit
	6	**Last day of class**
	8	**Final exam: 3–5:30 P.M.**

Freshman Seminar
US 1150-103
M-F 12:40 - 2:20 P.M.

Instructors: Dr. Dan Friedman	Peer Leader: Ms. Johnice Moore
E-mail: Office: 262-2028; 30 Whitener Hall	E-mail: Phone: peer leader phone number

PURPOSE

The purpose of this course is to help new college students make the transition from high school to college, both academically and socially. It aims to help students understand and meet the expectation and challenges of college and provides appropriate support and resources for students to be successful at ASU. It will help build academic and life skills, provide opportunities for personal growth, and establish new relationships.

GOALS

- *Develop intellectual and academic competence*

- *Establish and maintain interpersonal relationships (build community)*

- *Manage transition*

- *Broaden horizons and personal development*

- *Discover Appalachian*

EXPECTATIONS

We expect that students will attend every class session, participate in meaningful ways, keep an open mind, and respect the opinions of others. This promises to be an exciting, engaging, and fun learning experience.

TEXTS & MATERIALS

- ➤ *P.O.W.E.R. Learning,* 2nd Edition. Robert Feldman (Purchase at bookstore)
- ➤ *New Connections,* 4th Edition Friedman, Marsh, & Brantz (Purchase at bookstore)
- ➤ *Iron & Silk,* Mark Salzman (Summer Reading)
- ➤ *Calendar/Day Planner* (Purchase one of your choosing)
- ➤ *New York Times* (available free in residence hall)

OUT OF CLASS REQUIREMENTS

- ➤ GIC- (Wednesday, July 13, 12:40- 4:00 P.M.)
- ➤ One (1) Outdoor Program Activity
- ➤ Discover Appalachian Day (Saturday, July 9)
- ➤ Two (2) Cultural Events:
  - o July 9 at 8 P.M. An evening with Leahy (Farthing Auditorium)
  - o July 23 at 8 P.M. Ladysmith Black Mambazo (Farthing Auditorium)

GRADING:

100 pts.	Attendance & participation
50 pts.	E-mail journal (10 pts. each)
275 pts.	Papers

        -MBTI (100 pts.)
        -*Iron & Silk* (100 pts.)
        -*NY Times* Op-Ed (50 pts.)
        -Discover App. Day Reaction (25 pts.)

50 pts.	Quizzes

        -*NY Times*/Current Events (30 pts.)
        -Syllabus (10 pts.)
        -*Iron & Silk* (10 pts.)

75 pts.	Misc. assignments
25 pts.	Outdoor program trip
100 pts.	Wellness presentation
<u>100 pts.</u>	Final project
775	Total Points

GRADING SCALE:

93-100=A	90-92 = A-
88-89= B+	83-87= B
80-82= B-	78-79= C+
73-77= C	70-72= C-
68-69= D+	63-67= D
60-62= D-	Below 60= F

ATTENDANCE POLICY

You are expected to attend all class meetings and outside events. This is a seminar course in which attendance and participation are vital. Full credit will be given for perfect attendance. **Ten (10) points will be deducted from your attendance grade for each unexcused absence.** Also keep in mind that if you are not present, your participation grade will suffer. Summer school is a unique experience. Each summer class is the equivalent of two classes during the regular term. Therefore, with each absence you are missing twice the experience and work!

CULTURAL EVENTS & OUTDOOR PROGRAM

You will be required to attend two cultural events and one outdoor program during the semester. We will be attending the cultural events as a class (see above for listing of these events.) The final exam will ask for your reactions to these events.

E-MAIL JOURNAL:

You will be required to submit an e-mail journal as a means of reflective writing. You are required to send one e-mail entry per week. Entries for the week are due by **Sunday at midnight**. We will give you a topic/prompt every Friday in class.

    Your journal entries should demonstrate considerable reflection and thought. They should be at least two paragraphs long. Simply describing your weekend will not suffice. You must think deeply about the issues that are affecting your life. Studies show that first-year students who write in a journal cope more effectively with stress and are healthier than those who do not. In addition, the only way to enhance your writing ability is to practice. Thus, this journal will give you the outlet to reflect on your changing circumstances and to practice your writing. **Please send your entries to me (friedmandb@appstate.edu) and our peer leader (peerleaderemail@appstate.edu).**

PAPERS
Freshman Seminar is a writing (W) designated class. Therefore, you will be required to write several papers for this class. You will be graded on content, structure, grammar, and your ability to analyze or synthesize the material. All papers must be typed, double-spaced, and stapled. Please be sure to proofread your papers (or have someone else proofread them for you). Submitting papers with numerous typos or grammatical and spelling errors will significantly reduce your grade. The details for each paper will be handed out during the semester and will be posted on WebCT.

WELLNESS PRESENTATION
You will be divided into groups of three or four and be required to make an oral presentation on a wellness topic. Topics may include drugs, nutrition, safe sex/STD's, sleep, exercise, smoking, eating disorders, colds & flu, depression, and stress management. The presentations should be geared towards helping your fellow students. The presentations must be about 20 minutes in length, use PowerPoint, have at least **five** sources, include a bibliography and outline, have an interactive component to engage your audience, and conform to proper presentation guidelines (to be discussed in class later in the semester). All group members must be involved and are required to speak.

New York Times
You are being provided a unique and special opportunity this summer. You will receive—free of charge—a five-week (Monday-Friday) subscription to the *New York Times*. Being an educated person requires keeping up with current affairs; thus, we will be using the *Times* as a "text" in this class. You will be responsible for reading at least the front page articles and lead editorial every day (Monday-Friday). We expect that this will probably take about 30 minutes a day. Random current events quizzes will be given throughout the semester. You will also be asked to write one op-ed piece during the semester in response to an editorial. You should choose an editorial that resonates with you—something addressing an issue that you care about and excites you. Your op-ed should be no longer than 750 words. An example will be given during the semester.

Iron & Silk
Every year entering first year students at ASU engage in a shared scholarly pursuit by reading a common novel. This year's selection is *Iron and Silk*, written by Mark Salzman. We will be discussing this book over two class periods. You need to finish reading the book by Friday, July 22. You will be responsible for writing a paper on this book, which will be due July 29. More details will be provided later.

Appalachian State University
Freshman Seminar
U S 1150 134 4:00–6:45 pm Wednesday   143 D.D. Dougherty Building

Joni Webb Petschauer
Office: 100 D.D.Dougherty
262-3878 (office/leave message)
XXXX (home – call before 8 pm)
(petschaerjw@appstate.edu)
Peer Leader:

Academic Advisor:

History 1101 faculty member:

Dr. Francis T. Borkowski
Office: 421 Hayes School of Music
262-7537 (office)
(borkowskif@appstate.edu)

Emilie Guthrie –
    e-mail: peerleaderemail@appstate.edu
Marcia Gaskill –
    e-mail: gaskillmb@appstate.edu
Dr. Rene' Harder Horst – 262-7066
    e-mail: horstrh@appstate.edu

TEXTS:
New Connections: A Handbook for Freshman Seminar
P.O.W.E.R. Learning, Robert Feldman (rental system textbook)
Iron and Silk, Mark Salzman (summer reading selection)
ASU General Bulletin (received during orientation)
Advising Planner (received during orientation)

PURPOSE: Congratulations! You are a first year student in college and are among an elite group. Freshman Seminar is a course designed specifically for you with a goal of assisting you to make a successful transition from high school to university. As a member of a Freshman Learning Community, you have the unique opportunity to develop strong relationships with both students and faculty that will sustain you throughout your undergraduate career. During the course of the semester, we will engage in discussions regarding the reasons for a liberal education, the history and heritage of Appalachian, as well as develop a variety of academic success skills. It is our hope that we will provide a supportive group for one another and that the class will supply a provocative and stimulating agenda for your first semester as a university student.

PHILOSOPHY: We believe that successful students exhibit positive habits such as
1. Considering others feelings before speaking.
2. Arriving to class early and prepared.
3. Committing them to the creation of the very best work they can do.
4. Moving through their day with integrity.
5. Expecting and trusting your classmates to do their best work.

It is in practicing these habits that we indicate a value system that supports the individual character, which is necessary for a productive and useful society. We will view every aspect of this course through this filter of habits and values. We expect you to consider these qualities every time you act.

FORMAT: This course is a seminar that is part of a Freshman Learning Community. All of you should be taking Dr. Rene' Harder Horst's World Civilizations course that meets from 9:30-10:45 A.M. on Tuesday and Thursday.

A seminar differs from the typical lecture format of most introductory courses. You are expected to *read, experience, question, and reflect* on all activities we undergo as a class. At times, we will present information in a mini-lecture format or will invite a guest speaker to provide "expert knowledge" but this is not the norm. More often, we will participate in activities and conversations that assist you in creating a strong start to your undergraduate education. Therefore, **appropriate, positive, active participation, and attendance are necessary.**

GRADING: This course provides a grade for three hours of general elective credit (not social sciences or humanities credit). **You will receive** 1 (**W**)riting designator, 1 (**C**)omputer designator, and 1 (**C**)ross (**D**)iscipline designator. The grade you earn results from the *day-to-day effort* you display as well as the *cumulative reflection of your work on tests, papers, and projects*. As faculty, we struggle with ways to account for both student differences and faculty expectations. "Bell curve" and quotes do not bind us. If all students earn "A's," then all receive "A's." The same is true of "B's, C's, D's, and F's."

And there are some distinctions between these grades. It is easy to make a "C" in this course–it takes intentional and consistent effort to make higher or lower grades. **Please read the following descriptions and think about your work in these terms.**

An "A" reflects that a student made outstanding contributions to the success of the course. They participated in class, turned in all assignments on time, attended outside activities and excelled on tests, in written work and in discussions–their attendance record reflects that this class was among their highest commitments. They learned and they helped others to learn.

The grade of "B" reflects that a student was reliable, consistent, and positive with regular and solid contributions to the success of the course. Students who make "B's" sometimes miss a class and sometimes have perfect attendance. The work is always completed, they attend all activities, and they perform well on tests. It is the quality of their presence that distinguishes them from "A's" and "C's."

Students who earn "C's" come to class regularly (one or two absences) and participate often in class discussions and occasionally present important ideas and insights. They usually complete all but a few assignments on time, attend everything but sometimes refuse to accept responsibility for their own decisions. Overall, they are successful students with admirable goals.

Students who choose to make "D's" are often distinguished by a couple of "tardy" arrivals to class, occasional absences (because of other priorities), one or two contributions to class and a rather laissez-faire attitude towards the activities and assignments. They might do well on tests or they might do poorly. In other words, the individual does not make it a priority to be a member of our seminar.

The student who earns an "F" is detached and unwilling to change. We ask that students who believe they are in jeopardy of earning an "F" will meet with us as soon as they recognize this concern and see if we can come with a strategy to avoid this grade.

By the way, we assign "+ and -"s as they are appropriate.

REQUIREMENTS: You are required to attend all classes and activities (cultural/outdoor events are among these required activities). This is the first tool of academic success. Your final grade will be lowered for missing more than three hours of class.

IF YOU MISS AN HOUR OR ANY PART OF AN HOUR OF CLASS, IT WILL COUNT AS ONE OF THE THREE HOURS OF CLASS. These hours should be used for family emergencies and illness–I strongly recommend that you bank them for emergencies rather than spend them frivolously. For example, if you have a final grade of a B and you have four hours of absences, you will receive a B-; if you have five hours of absences, you will receive a C+, and so forth. Any emergency absences should be explained immediately (e-mail or call one of us). If there is an "in-class" assignment on a day that you miss, you will receive a "0" for that assignment. If it is an assignment that can or needs to be made up for your success with future assignments (not a quiz), then we will consider grading your make-up work and averaging that grade with the "0." By no means should you assume that you can "make-up" a missed assignment.

You can expect the following activities and assignments to be used to determine your grade. The points listed are the maximum that can be earned by completing a particular assignment.

- class attendance (on time) and participation (enthusiastic, contributing, and prepared) (10%) **BEWARE–JUST SHOWING UP DOES NOT GUARANTEE THAT YOU WILL RECEIVE A POINT**
- attendance at and participation in the following activities *when they are scheduled on the syllabus or determined by the class*
  - Campus Resource Tour (5%)
  - Walk for Awareness (5%)
  - Convocation (5%)
  - Group Interaction Course (5%)
  - Campus Cultural Events (10%)
  - Service Learning Project (5%)
  - Parent Interview (5%)
  - Library Tutorial (5%)
  - Apple iMovie Project – team and/or attendance at premier (5%)
- 2 papers–with revisions (20%). Additional guidelines for these writing assignments will be provided when they are assigned.
  Paper 1–What does it mean to be an educated person? What behaviors, language, values, attitudes, and experiences are associated with someone who is educated? What role does a university experience play in the education of citizens? Who do you know and consider to be an educated person?

Paper 2–What needs to be included in a university education? What courses, skills, experiences, and expectations would you require? Research the requirements of other campuses and compare these to Appalachian's requirements. What ideas would you recommend Appalachian keep, and what ideas would you take from other campuses?

Nothing can be turned in after Thanksgiving with the exception of admit cards and your final project. It is critical for you to do your own work. Do not collaborate with others on your papers, even if you attended the event together. We realize that such assignments seem simple enough and yet, we require a tightly organized, creative and insightful response. Our goal is not to be difficult but rather to give you significant experience addressing issues such as this so that you may improve your writing skills for essay questions and "job reports."

There are no extra credit assignments. We hope you will spend your time working on the above activities rather than seeking extra credit assignments to make up work you missed.

COURSE TOPICS AND OUTLINE: There are several topics that we believe are important to this course but there is a great degree of flexibility regarding the order of presentation. We will seek your input as to the order of things to come, based on your needs and knowledge. Below is a *tentative* course outline:

Wednesday (8/24)	Introduction to our course and ourselves; Expectations and Responsibilities; *The Atlantic Slave Trade*; Boundary Breaking; Paper 1 Assignment: What does it mean to be an educated person? (5 pages–due 9/7)
Wednesday (8/31)	Walk for Awareness video; GROUP INTERACTION COURSE meet in classroom at 4 P.M. Activity: 4:30-8:30. Class is extended on this day.
Tuesday (9/6)	**WALK FOR AWARENESS—MEET ON SANFORD MALL-9 P.M.**
Wednesday (9/7)	Convocation; Campus Resource Tour information; Work on History exam questions
Thursday (9/8)	**CONVOCATION—Meet in front of the John E. Thomas Building (with the two flames) and walk with Emily to the Convocation Center at 9:40 A.M. REQUIRED ATTENDANCE.** The ceremony will begin at 10:00 A.M. in Varsity Gym. Classes are cancelled from 8-12:30 P.M. so that the academic community can attend. You are required to attend this event for this class. The speaker is Mark Salzman–the author of the summer reading book, *Iron and Silk*.

<u>**Tuesday (9/13)**</u>	**Open House and Campus Resource Tour–5:25 P.M. meet in Lobby of D.D. Dougherty (5:30-6:50 P.M.)**
Wednesday (9/14)	Time Management; NT; Service Learning Introduction; History Test; Rewrites due for Paper 1
<u>**Saturday (9/17)**</u>	**THE RIVER SWEEP–OUR SERVICE PROJECT**
Wednesday (9/21)	Learning Styles; Debrief the River Sweep; Alcohol Awareness; TT
Wednesday (9/28)	Library Tutorial; *The Shawnee Prophet*; Parent Interview; Assignment: What should be included in a college education? (5 pages—due 10/19)
Wednesday (10/5) Auditorium	**United States Marine Corps Band 8 P.M.–Farthing**
Wednesday (10/12)	Academic advising with Marcia; study abroad; library tour
Wednesday (10/19)	Appalachian history; conducting
Wednesday (10/26)	Roommates; values; registration; *Lest Innocent Blood Be Shed*
Wednesday (11/2)	**Jazz Concert 8 P.M.–Rosen Concert Hall**
Wednesday (11/9)	Class hike and dinner at Frank's; discussion about book
Wednesday (11/16)	The Meaning of an Undergraduate Education; Rewrites due for Paper 2
Wednesday (11/30)	Schedule adjustment with Marcia; last class

OUR FINAL EXAM PERIOD IS TUESDAY, DECEMBER 13 FROM 12-2:30 P.M.

STRATEGIES FOR ENGAGING STUDENTS—PROMISING PRACTICES

In "Our Teaching Philosophy," we have shared what we believe to be the essence of good teaching. Building academic community is at the heart of that philosophy. To build that community, instructors should focus on ways to use course content that will promote an active demonstration of knowledge by their students.

It is a goal of this Instructor's Manual to provide you with a variety of teaching techniques and ideas to enhance the learning process of your students. "Teaching the Text" is devoted to chapter-by-chapter notes that suggest ways to engage your students in the active process of learning and building an academic community.

Pay particular attention to four sections in "Teaching the Text," which provide activities and thoughts about teaching:

- Section IV.   Classroom Activities and Assignments
- Section V.   Using the P.O.W.E.R. Learning Process in Your Instruction
- Section VII.   Continuing the Conversation Beyond the Classroom
- Section VIII.   Classroom Activities to Support Teaching This Chapter

Bob Feldman states early in the *P.O.W.E.R. Learning* text "good students are made, not born." So, too, can this statement be applied to teachers? There is an extensive body of literature in higher education about the importance of actively engaging students in learning. Several practices have been identified as showing great promise in making a positive difference in the learning outcomes of students. Among the most promising practices are:

- learning communities
- undergraduate research
- service learning
- internationalization
- summer readings and/or common books

Student success courses can play an integral role in expanding the presence of these pedagogies throughout a campus and it is vital to consider how to incorporate them within the context of your course. Following is a brief description of each of these ideas.

Learning Communities

Learning communities provide a programmatic structure for bringing together students, faculty, and educational support team members who desire to learn specific skills, explore similar interests, and solve common problems. By co-enrolling small groups of interested students in selected courses, students have an opportunity to integrate class material more fully while meeting individuals and learning about resources and services that will support their academic efforts. Through their course faculty, these students make connections to academic departments that support their professional goals; through their academic support team (advisors, librarians, peer leaders, and/or tutors), they make connections to services that support their academic success; and through student affairs professionals, there are opportunities to connect the co-curricular activities to curricular goals. Learning communities provide a structure for using all of the resources on a campus for achieving learning goals.

Student success courses are an excellent choice to serve as anchor courses in first-year learning communities. The skills and content associated with success courses can be taught in the context of other curricular offerings and since the coursework is taken in common with other students, it makes for natural comparisons and accelerated learning. Teaching study skills without an academic context is not compelling for college students. Teaching academic content without the necessary skills for managing the information is often too challenging for first year students to handle. Connecting the two—content and skills—reflects an ideal mix of challenge and support.

Undergraduate Research

The goal of undergraduate research is to enrich the undergraduate experience through high quality collaborative research and scholarship. Such programs enhance campus teaching and learning efforts by providing students with firsthand experience of scholarly exploration, discovery, and application. This can, in turn, make the classroom experience more meaningful because students can more fully appreciate the academic life of faculty and faculty can more readily recognize the various modes of inquiry and knowing that students bring into their courses. One of the great challenges of a campus that focuses on undergraduate education is providing faculty with the opportunity to be active in creative and scholarly activities beyond teaching classes. Undergraduate research programs provide a venue for this to occur while encouraging faculty-student mentoring. It is common for these programs to sponsor a showcase event for faculty and students to present their findings or share their creations as well as provide support for teams to attend conference or participate in publications.

The role of student success courses or Freshman Seminars with undergraduate research is multifold. At a research focused or small liberal arts institution, the Freshman Seminar might be a fully developed undergraduate research course with a small group of students working with a senior faculty member on a specific research or creative interest. At a comprehensive institution or community college, it might provide an introduction to the concept of undergraduate research and require the development of a proposal for a future undergraduate project. Such an assignment would assume that students would become familiar with the campus library and other resources that would support the project's completion.

Service Learning

Volunteerism through community service has long been a common practice in university life. In recent years, this activity has been directly linked to educational outcomes and has come to be known as service learning. Students find this direct application of knowledge and skills learned in the classroom to real-life situations outside the classroom to be an exciting way to learn. Service learning is distinguished from volunteerism because it includes the three-step process of 1) preparation, 2) action, and 3) reflection, which supports its integration into classroom teaching and learning goals.

Service learning provides a heightened level of interaction with faculty as well as with community agencies and individuals. Students who have been involved in service-learning classes report a greater sense of civic engagement, a clearer understanding of their community, and enhancement of skills needed for future careers (particularly in the area of leadership development). Service learning is an excellent tool to use in a first year student course, connecting first-time students to faculty and community with this engaging pedagogy.

Internationalizing the Campus/Curriculum

Study abroad is often the first thing that comes to mind when the phrase "internationalizing the campus/curriculum" is mentioned and yet so much preparation is needed before we can consider putting the first student on a plane. We must ensure that the campus environment embraces diversity, encourages dialogues, and holds individuals responsible for being global citizens. We should encourage students to explore course offerings that teach a different perspective, speak a new language, or study an intriguing culture.

Few experiences, however, capture the international experience as completely as study abroad opportunities. Begin the introduction to this possibility during the first year. Encourage students to share the desire to study abroad with academic advisors as they plan their course of study. Invite international students studying on your campus to your class to share their experience and introduce their country and culture in a personal way.

Preparing student to live and work in a multi-ethnic, global society is our responsibility.

Summer Reading/Common Book Programs

By participating in a Summer Reading or Common Book program, students establish a common experience with other new students that will help develop a sense of community with their new environment and introduce them to a part of the academic life they are beginning on their college campus. Connecting a common reading to co-curricular activities such as films, speakers, convocation or graduation ceremonies, concerts, and theater performances can enhance the academic climate. Connecting such a book to general education courses or major specific classes can generate deeper learning outcomes. Most importantly, such programs send the message that reading is an important part of the educational experience.

STUDENT ASSESSMENT

Assessing students with traditional grades in Freshman Seminar courses is a difficult task. The very nature of this course does not lend itself to the standard testing procedures. As we move to consider the learning outcomes in assessment, it is important to consider such measures as: portfolios, capstone projects, and work that speaks to creative endeavors.

Throughout the "Teaching the Text: Chapter-by-Chapter Notes," we suggest using methods such as a variety of assignments that evaluate writing (admit/exit card, journal reflections), group work, presentations, and others as they seem appropriate. Additionally, we want you to know about other ways to learn more about how your students think and how they can articulate what they know. We are particularly appreciative of those assessment activities that allow students to practice their developing skills on a daily basis. In this section, you will find:

- Example of Regular Review
- Examples of Final Exam Options
- Examples of Closure Activities

STUDENT ASSESSMENT: EXAMPLE OF REGULAR REVIEW

The Informal Quiz
(developed by Supplemental Instruction at the University of Missouri at Kansas City)

1. Use scrap paper or half sheets.

2. Move quickly through the quiz.

3. Ask a majority of questions requiring short answers.

4. If there are students who aren't writing answers, say "If you don't know the answer, write the question so that you will remember what it was you didn't know."

5. Compose a maximum of ten questions.

6. Questions should be comprehensive, covering concepts the instructor want the students to understand.

7. Questions on familiar material can be varied, i.e., the following:

   a. "The answer is _____; what is the question?"
   b. "I can't think of any more. Does any one have a question I might ask?"

8. Most questions should not be difficult, but should emphasize recall of key points or of minor points related to key points. One or perhaps two questions should require use of higher-order thinking skills.

9. In answering questions, be sure to ask who would like to answer a question–any questions. When calling on students, ask something like, "Which question do you wish to answer or have answered?"

10. Call on the weakest students first, whenever they have raised a hand.

11. Restate the question before the answer is given.

12. Don't argue if someone wants to answer a question that has already been answered. Students will protest; teacher can say, "Just because the question has been answered doesn't mean it has been used up."

13. Find something complimentary to say about wrong answers, like "That's a very good guess. If I weren't sure I might have guessed that."

14. Keep it light and short.

STUDENT ASSESSMENT: EXAMPLES OF FINAL EXAM OPTIONS

The Symbolic Gift

Our final exam provides an opportunity for each of you to present the most powerful idea, concept, and/or tool which you believe next year's first year students need to have in their possession to coming on campus.

Look at the syllabus, go through your notes, and consider your journal entries and our class discussions as you decide your gift to the class. You are expected to give a nine- to ten-minute presentation, which is informative and engaging. Furthermore, you are to create or find a physical token for the idea/concept/tool that you intend to give. Poems are fine, provided they are your own, are meaningful and not "sappy." I have always been impressed by the creativity students have expressed in their gifts. One student gave the class a pair of wings (she made them and brought them in) and shared an inspirational quote and spoke to the events in her life and the experiences in the course that made this appropriate. Another student gave the class a "one act play" which she wrote, directed, and acted for us. Another student gave the class a painting entitled "during your first year, you will discover what color you are" and she discussed how and why she was lavender.

There are no limits to your gift except the time in which you give it and making sure there is some physical symbol that can be left behind for me to show next year's class. (If you paint a symbol. … be prepared to leave it.)

Grading: Each of you will be given a specific set of criteria by which you will evaluate one another and yourself. I will provide a third evaluation. I will tally each of these scores, divide by three, and this will be your grade on this final.

Mission Statement
(developed by Dr. Randy Swing)

Develop a mission statement and goals for your college experience using the following steps:

1. Using 3 × 5 index cards, brainstorm possible outcomes of a college education (how you will change, what you will learn, skills you will develop. improve, etc.). Next, sort related items into groups and add additional cards as new ideas arise. Type an edited list to submit as part of the final assignment. NOTE: You are encouraged to form groups to accomplish this task. When a group performs work, it is appropriate that names of all group members be noted on the final product.

2. Create an academic SWOT analysis (Strengths, Weaknesses, Opportunities, and Threats). For this assignment, focus on SWOTs that directly impact your success in college. Review the following materials from our class discussions:

>The Freshman Seminar Textbook
>Institutional Mission Statement
>18 goals for an undergraduate education
>Weekly reaction cards

>Your SWOT analysis should follow this format:

Internal Environment (Who I am)

STRENGTHS	WEAKNESSES
Strengths that lead to academic success	Academic skills you need to develop

External Environment (Institution, Family, the World)

OPPORTUNITIES	THREATS
What is available or will become so	What will hold you back or limit your progress

3. Building from Step 2, write at least 15 goals for your college career. These goals might utilize strengths or overcome weaknesses. Goals should be realistic.

4. The last step is to write a personal mission statement for your college career. This will combine your goals, SWOT analysis, and personal ideas about higher education.

The Final Exam: A Letter to Next Year's First Year Students

General Instructions. The final examination in this course will be a letter to next fall's class. What are the formal instructions?

1) The letter must be dated.
2) It must begin "Dear 2___ (appropriate year) First Year Student"
3) It may not exceed two typed pages.
4) You must sign it.
5) It is due at the final exam period.
6) It must include a discussion of the following items.

1. **Introduction.** You should introduce yourself to next year's first year student, explaining briefly where you are from, what high school you attended, what you liked best about high school, why you chose this campus, and what you are planning to study or major in on our campus. In addition, I want you to explain one or two new things that you have discovered about yourself during this semester.

2. **Transitions.** Next, I want you to explain what for you were the most difficult transitions in your move from high school to college. You might want to focus on life in the residence halls, meeting new people, roommates, adjusting to college classroom expectations, managing your time, elevated stress levels, money management, etc. In the process, note ways in which the college, fellow students, Freshman Seminar, parents, or faculty who have helped you make transitions.

3. **Discovering Our Campus**. Another goal of our course has been to discover the full range of educational opportunities, university, support services, and institutional history. I would like you to briefly explain to next fall's first year students the most important things that you have learned about our campus in these categories.

4. **Learning Strategies**. I would also like you to explain which learning strategies that we studied this semester helped you the most (no more than three). Also explain how you plan to make use of them next semester.

5. **Broadening Horizons**. Throughout the semester we have explored new areas and broadened our horizons, especially in the cultural area. I would like you to explain how one of the cultural events we attended this semester broadened your horizons. Included in this section should be a comment about why cultural events are considered such an important part of a university education and how they bring different academic disciplines together into a single experience.

6. **Becoming an Independent Learner**. Finally, I would like you to explain three or four ways in which you have changed or risked change over this past month. (This could be personally, academically, socially, in attitudes toward college, feelings toward your family, understanding of what it means to be an educated person, etc.) Have you become an independent learner in the process? Why or why not?

Please write your letter in an easy friendly style, paying attention to correct spelling, grammar, and so on. Illustrate your general statements with examples whenever possible, utilize logical transitions from one topic to another, keep the entire letter in essay form, and try to be as concise and clear in your comments as possible.

STUDENT ASSESSMENT: EXAMPLES OF CLOSURE ACTIVITIES

The final meeting of Freshman Seminar is as important as the opening day. On the first day you introduced yourself and your goals, modeled your class format, and sold students on the value of Freshman Seminar. Now it's time to remind students of what they have learned and experienced, of what they have done and how far they have come. It is time for a powerful closure, one that fits with your class and personal style, one that sums up or expresses your collective experiences. No single closure is right for every class, but as you prepare for closure during your final examination period, you might want to consider one or more of the activities listed below. Closure activities may or may not be graded but any time students synthesize their experience, you will find yourself making judgments about their thinking. These closure activities have worked for faculty in the past, and they might trigger new ideas or twists that will work in your class.

The Hot Seat

This is a sharing activity designed to reinforce a sense of community, mutual trust, caring, and lasting communications. The instructions set a serious tone for this exercise, encouraging everyone to remain involved and be honest in his or her participation. The class sits in a circle with a chair (swivel chair preferably) in the center. Each student is then invited to sit in the "Hot Seat." The person has 60 seconds (longer or shorter if you want) to say anything he or she wants to say to the class or any individual in the class. The rest of the class must remain silent and listen to the comments. Then for two to three minutes anyone in the class can say anything he or she would like to the person in the "Hot Seat" and that person cannot respond. Extroverts will volunteer first, but eventually even the quietest and most reserved member of the class will step forward. The experience may be most powerful for those who wait to the last, so don't let anyone off or hurry the final participants. It is a powerful closure experience.

Good-Bye Tapes

Students create relationships in Freshman Seminar that go beyond those created in more subject-oriented classes. Acknowledging the "end" to class relationships in a personal way reminds students of the need to say good-bye to other friends, family, and classmates. By showing the endings to several popular movies (*Big Fish, Garden State*, etc.), you can set the stage for a very powerful discussion of what it means to say good-bye. It provides a fitting setting for reviewing and evaluating what the classes and student relationships mean. Allowing good-byes to be said also gives strength to the concept of saying hello in the future.

Mail Box

This activity involves each student writing a note to all other students in the class expressing their thanks, thoughts, or wishes for that person. This takes about 40 minutes and can be done in conjunction with other closure activities or evaluations. Faculty members should encourage students to read these notes immediately and then put them away to be read later. The final expression is a powerful way for students to remember each person in class.

Symbolic Gifts

Each member of the class prepares a fantasy gift (object, values, people, ideas, etc.) for everyone in class or for next year's first year students. They may present these or some tangible symbol of this gift to others in the class. They may be asked to stand in front of the person to whom they are giving these symbolic gifts and hold eye contract with them during the process. This closure activity allows students to be as creative as they want. Some prompting and suggestions from the instructor can help get things going. You may even want to liven it up by creating a mythical "fountain of gifts" in the center of the room from which these symbolic gifts can be drawn and delivered.

Becoming

In this closure activity, students are given paper and pencils and are instructed to write their first names in large block letters on top of their piece of paper. Then they are asked to complete the following sentence in as many ways as they can: "I am becoming a person who…" When everyone has finished, students mill around silently, reading each other's sheets, then leave.

Eye Contact Circle

The group stands in a circle and one member goes around the circle in a clockwise direction, establishing eye contact and verbally communicating one way with each person. The student returns to his place so that each class member can tell the student something. Having the second person follow the first around the circle can speed up the design, the third follow the second, etc.

Meaningful Quotes

In this activity, class members select one or two meaningful quotes from *Whisper of the River* (or whatever book they read), and explain why the quotes are so meaningful to them.

Personal Mission Statement

In this exercise, started the last week of the semester, students are asked to develop their own personal academic mission statements (similar to those in the long-range plan and college catalog). During the final period students share their mission statements.

Your Last Statement

Each member of the class is asked to present a short statement about himself or herself. Assume that this is the last thing he or she would ever be able to say. The result is a powerful statement of who the student thinks he or she is at this point in life.

As the above suggest, there are numerous ways to organize closure in Freshman Seminar. Many faculty put several activities together to achieve the kind of closing they are after. Some combine a going-away party, film, and other activities. Others try to join the "Hot Seat" and "Good-Bye" films. Still others collect final projects, have a final exam, administer student evaluations, or use the session for debriefing or feedback. Whatever approach you are planning, make it as effective and as powerful as your opening day.

COURSE EVALUATION

Constant evaluation offers the only way to find out if students are learning what we are teaching. Freshman Seminar instructors often adjust their course direction based on mid-term or end-of-the-semester evaluations. Course evaluations provide the Freshman Seminar office with indicators of what is working and what needs attention. Knowing the nature of the required course evaluation also provides instructors with the criteria on which they will be evaluated. Finally, evaluations from past years remind us of how successful Freshman Seminar instructors have been from year to year, and they set a standard for future classes. Following you will find:

- examples of midterm evaluations
- example of a final course evaluation

Midterm Evaluation (Example 1)

I. Purpose of Midterm Evaluation

It is always wise to start an evaluation with a purpose. Doing an evaluation just for the sake of an evaluation makes little sense. Once you arrive at a purpose, then you can begin to evaluate whether you have reached that purpose. One central purpose might be to improve the course. This might include determining how effective the course is for the students. Is it meeting their needs, assisting them in other classes, helping them become independent learners, and instilling confidence in their ability to succeed? Or the purpose of the evaluation might be to elicit suggestions about how you could be a more effective instructor. Or you might want to simply encourage students to give more honest feedback.

Whatever your purpose for evaluating at midterm, one technique that is guaranteed to produce powerful results is the midterm evaluation. It can be a little risky, but it can also be a very powerful way of allowing students to buy into your course for the second half of the semester. It can give you honest, open feedback and the opportunity to demonstrate your confidence in the class.

II. Procedure

1.   Using 3×5 index cards or in an email or web portal, ask students to list anonymously two things—topics and activities— that they particularly like about the course.

2.   Using another card, ask students to list anonymously two things that they don't like about the course: instructor, activities, atmosphere, assignments, workload, grading, etc.

3.   Collect the cards or compile the comments and read the non-repetitive comments to the class, making certain to devote about as much time to the complaints as to the positive statements. The key to the success of this kind of evaluation will be reading candid criticisms of yourself and your class out loud without commenting or responding or seeming to dismiss student comments as trivial. Perhaps a nod, an acknowledgment of its importance will suffice; in some cases, probably no comment will be best. This amounts to your recognition before the entire class that you are interested in their feedback that you are listing.

4.   The final step is to ask students for assistance in developing the course agenda for the rest of the semester. Using 3×5 index cards again (or whatever platform works for you), ask students to list two to three things that they need. Ask them how this can be delivered most effectively. Be certain to read some of the suggestions out loud to the class and incorporate a few of them openly into your class schedule for the second part of the semester. (You might prep them for this part of the exercise by raising a number of questions that invite comment. For example, should your teaching style be varied? Are ideas being communicated effectively? Should the class be more interactive? Would more guest speakers be appropriate? Are more in-class demonstrations needed? Is more time needed for sharing, conversation, or feedback? Is the workload overwhelming? Do students understand the grading system outlined in the syllabus? There are numerous kinds of questions that you can develop that will elicit helpful feedback. The results will probably be open and honest because of your willingness to look in a straightforward manner at their reactions to the class.)

III. Results

What this kind of evaluation provides is a class temperature at midterm. It also offers an opportunity to build additional trust and openness with the class. This kind of open-ended evaluation will not serve as a definitive guide for reconstructing a syllabus, but it can provide you with an idea of where students are, how they view the course, and what their expectations are for the semester.

Midterm Evaluation (Example 2)

II. Response Card

Your honest evaluation is requested. Please help me understand how to make this an outstanding experience for you and future students.

How has the teacher made this class boring/interesting?	What contribution have you made to keep this class interesting?	How have the other students made the class boring/interesting?

How much and how has/has not the teacher shown care and concern for you?	What have you done to acquaint yourself with the teacher and "used" him/her to get what you want from Freshman Seminar?

Is grading policy clear and fair? Or not?	I have/have not reviewed the class syllabus lately and do/do not track my grades.

State one important thing you have learned from this class.

State one important thing you still wish to get from this class.

Midterm Evaluation (Example 3)

III. Student/Faculty Evaluation

Rate each of the following:

SA	A	D	SD
Strongly Agree	Agree	Disagree	Strongly Disagree

TEACHER   **ME**

_____   Comes to class prepared   _____

_____   Considers this class important   _____

_____   Has made an effort to make the class fun   _____

_____   Works at keeping class from being boring   _____

_____   Gives energy to the class assignments   _____

Final Course Evaluation

Indicate the degree to which the following statements are descriptive of your experience in this course. Use the following scale:

A-Strongly Agree   B-Agree   C-Neutral   D-Disagree   E-Strongly Disagree

1. I entered college with well-developed and effective study skills.

2. This course increased my knowledge of services available to assist students.

3. This course helped me develop effective time management skills.

4. This course helped me develop new friendships with other first year students.

5. This course introduced me to cultural and artistic activities.

6. This course helped me understand the goals of a college education.

7. This course helped me take responsibility for my education and my personal growth.

8. Freshman Seminar helped me improve study skills

9. This course has increased my knowledge of the history of our institution.

10. I would recommend this course to other first year students.

11. The instructor was well prepared for class.

12. Grading was fair and clearly explained.

13. Course material was appropriate for this class.

14. I felt comfortable discussing questions and problems in class.

15. The instructor showed caring and concern for me.

16. I learned to use e-mail, word processing and web-based instruction in Freshman Seminar.

17. I visited the Freshman Seminar home page.

18. Word processing and basic computing skills are important academic skills.

19. The computer lab is an adequate facility.

20. I completed one or more written papers and received feedback.

21. I applied skills and information learned in Freshman Seminar to other courses.

Optional

If your class had a peer leader, please answer the following:

22. My peer leader made important contributions to our class.

If your class participated in a service project, please answer the following:

23. Volunteering in the community is important.

24. Participation in a service project was a valuable component of my Freshman Seminar component.

If your class was part of a linked course or learning community experience, please answer the following:

25. Being co-enrolled in two or more courses with a group of classmates has led to relationships
    that support my academic success.

26. I would recommend a learning community experience to other first year students.

Please comment on each of the following questions. Write your answers on this page in the space provided.

What activities and experiences did you find most valuable in this course?

What activities and experiences did you find least valuable in this course?

What suggestions do you have for changing or improving this course?

Please comment on your instructor's strengths and weaknesses.

III

IMPLICATIONS FOR BROADER FACULTY

DEVELOPMENT ON YOUR CAMPUS

Overview

Student success courses provide a unique opportunity to address and define what it means to be a member of a specific campus. Over 80% of American institutions of higher education provide some type of "extended orientation" course for its students. The primary purpose of such a course is to craft a common language and create a shared understanding for students and faculty to interact with one another.

Given the diversity of American secondary educational experiences and the increased access to postsecondary educational opportunities, it is easy to understand the importance of being explicit about the responsibilities and expectations of all involved. Obviously, student success leads to conversations about the teaching/learning mission of a campus, and thus it is ideal for such courses to be developed with widespread faculty input and considerable administrative support.

Course and/or Program Leadership

Every campus is different. First and foremost, successful implementation of a student success course or program requires administrative coordination. Someone or some group must be responsible for establishing the goals, articulating the purpose, recruiting and preparing the faculty, and reporting the experiences of the students. On some campuses, recruiting students is also a primary responsibility of this person/group/office, but on other campuses, this responsibility belongs to students, academic advisors, and orientation leaders. Small committees or work teams, respected faculty facilitators, and/or talented administrators have led successful programs. Keep in mind that student success is not a specific academic discipline but rather a cross-disciplinary philosophy that focuses on the learning process. The articulation of this philosophy on your campus must honestly reflect the concerns and values under which you work. These courses often encourage a review and reshaping of policies that affect student retention and success. Your administrative leadership should be selected with this idea in mind.

Recruiting Faculty

There are many ways to identify, prepare, and reward individuals involved with the development and teaching of student success courses, and being sensitive to what works on your campus is paramount to the creation of a sustainable program. Consider using more than one recruitment approach and be open to a variety of ideas.

It is always an expected practice to promote the course and its development through official lines by informing chief administrative officers, deans, chairs, faculty governance boards, and so on. Not only should you seek out and individually invite faculty members who have excellent reputations for teaching, but also, you should be open to those faculty members who are interested in trying out new ideas in order to enhance their teaching reputations. Courses outside of a department provide a safe place for experimenting with new ways of teaching.

Develop brochures and materials that not only answer questions and state goals for students but also consider creating similar materials for faculty and other members of your academic community. Consider holding a luncheon or breakfast at the end of each semester for teaching faculty to share their successes with one another; encourage each of these faculty members to bring a colleague with them to this meal. Ask departmental chairs, deans, students, and staff to recommend faculty members from whom they would enjoy learning. Remember that individuals who might want to pursue teaching this course may need to know that others consider them appropriate for the task. Indeed, while films and textbooks often cast faculty members as arrogant and overly confident, most college professors are extremely approachable and truly concerned about their teaching. It is one thing to be certain of and an expert in one's field of research . . . it is another to be confident about teaching that field.

Finally, be open to having individuals on your campus who are not traditional faculty members as potential members of your instructional team. Excellent programs throughout the nation include discipline-specific faculty members, academic advisors, student development professionals, residence life staff, athletic coaches, administrators, secretaries, and a variety of other university staff members; it takes the effort of an entire academic community to teach the message of student success. In order for the program to be truly sustainable, however, you must make certain that traditional faculty generate, facilitate, and shape the curriculum. Otherwise, the course will not be integrated or accepted as "the real work of higher education."

Rewarding Faculty ("You get what you pay for")

Student success courses have the potential to increase student retention, to revitalize faculty-teaching efforts, to refocus conversations on your campus, to provide opportunities for cross-departmental discussions and support, and for any number of other positive outcomes. It stands to reason then that establishing a reward structure will most likely ensure that your campus reaps the best of these outcomes. Since this course is not taught in a traditional department, upper-level administrators need to implement the reward structure, and they should be entirely comfortable with working "outside the normal path."

Ways to reward faculty include:
- contract extensions/pay for participation in training workshop(s)
- reassigned time for teaching
- contract extensions/pay for teaching course
- travel funds
- research material funds
- credit towards reassigned time for research
- new equipment (computers, smart classrooms, etc.) and training
- first pick at classroom space and/or teaching times for their departmental commitments

Departments can be encouraged to support their faculty in these efforts through:
- additional travel funds for departmental members
- additional graduate assistants/teaching assistants
- additional funds for departmental supplies/services/functions
- additional funds to be used as incentives (raises, etc.) for faculty who participate in institutional efforts, such as teaching outside the department
- specific reference to this important work in promotion and tenure documents

The bottom line is that these courses support the institutional mission of teaching and learning, and it behooves a campus to openly and generously support the efforts of the faculty involved in them.

Faculty Preparation and Training

As much as possible, faculty training for student success courses should mirror the course itself. In other words, do not expect faculty members to carry out ideas that you have not modeled.

A good example of this would be using the Group Interaction Course (GIC) or Low Ropes Initiatives. Once faculty members experience this activity as a group during a training period, they will be more likely to understand its power as an educational tool and thus, will be more willing to use it in their teaching. The same is true with specific teaching techniques that encourage discussion and promote reflection; it is important for instructors to experience the outcome of these ideas. Most faculty members do not delve into personal issues when teaching within their normal academic discipline. Thus, in a class such as this, when students begin to trust their classmates and their teacher, it is common for a different level of disclosure to develop. Preparing faculty to deal with more intimate conversation in their classrooms is vital to the success of this course. Following is an example of a weeklong student success course faculty-training workshop. An excellent time to provide this workshop would be following spring semester graduation in preparation for fall semester teaching. It is not recommended to provide this workshop during a week immediately prior to the semester the faculty will be teaching this course.

**Week-Long Schedule
for a Freshman Seminar Faculty Training Workshop**

Monday (Goals: Begin to build community among training participants; role model discussions, mini-lectures, and guest lecturers. Illustrate how "breaking bread together" is a simple way to extend the idea of community beyond the classroom; show importance of breaks and assignments.)

8:45	Gathering with coffee and refreshments
9:00	Welcome and overview of workshop and materials (text, manual, etc.)
9:15	Introductions
9:45	Boundary Breaking
10:45	Break
11:00	Discussion/activity: "What Do Our Students Need to Be Successful in College?" List of needs generated by workshop participants based on what they have observed in their classes.
11:25	Mini-lecture: "National Research Findings about American College Students"
11:55	Identify small groups and assign presentation topics for Thursday
12:00	Lunch together—Dutch treat at local restaurant
1:15	Discussion and mini-lecture: "What Is Community, Why Is It Important, How Do We Build It?"
2:00	Guest lecturer: "National Efforts at Improving Student Success"
4:00	Dismiss

Assignment:
1.   Read article about student development theory
2.   Answer questions on learning styles inventory and bring with you tomorrow
3.   Think about the following topic: Outcomes-based education – The shift is here. How can this course help our campuses respond?

Reminder:
Dress appropriately for participation in GIC tomorrow.

Tuesday (Goals: Introduce student development theory as a foundation for understanding how college students learn; role model teaching techniques that enhance discussion and thoughtful reflection; continue to use guest lecturers to provide expert knowledge. Conduct the GIC as a common learning experience that can be referred to throughout the week.)

8:45	Gathering with coffee and refreshments
9:00	Review yesterday's experiences/ preview today's activities
9:00	Guest lecturer: "Student Development/Learning Theory"
10:00	Activity and discussion of student development/learning theory (break taken as needed)
11:30	Guest lecturer: "What Our Institution Knows about Our Students' Needs"
12:00	Lunch (provided by workshop so that participants can leave "on time for GIC")
1:00	Group Interaction Course (away from workshop classroom)
4:00	Dismiss

Assignment:
Write an admit card based on GIC experience; respond to prompt:
1.   How can this activity be used to support the academic goals I have for my students?
2.   Bring your favorite potluck dish for lunch tomorrow.

Reminder:
Group presentations are on Thursday!

Wednesday (Goals: Provide specific information about skills and concepts that students need to know to be successful learners; use textbook as an important resource for information; introduce resources available for teaching this course—audiovisual equipment, secretarial support, funds, computers, etc.)

8:45	Gathering with coffee and refreshments
9:00	Review yesterday's experiences/preview today's activities
9:05	Interactive review of textbook topics and Instructor's Manual; specifically illustrate ways to teach learning skills; familiarize participants with instructional materials
10:15	Break
10:30	Guest lecturer "Learning Styles Inventories"; teaching and learning as it relates to different styles
12:00	Lunch (potluck at program director's home—invite former faculty)

1:40	Nuts and Bolts—additional instructional resources and how to use them computer labs, smart classroom and white board office copier, overhead projector, peer leaders, secretarial support, VCR, monitor, and videos
3:30	Midweek (midterm) evaluation
	Group conferences for tomorrow's presentations
4:00	Dismiss

Thursday (Goals: Continue to highlight student success tools such as writing, speaking; participants become experts during the group presentations; introduce offices/services/ programs throughout the institutional community that support student success.)

8:45	Gathering with coffee and refreshments
9:00	Review midweek evaluation responses
9:05	Demonstrate "fishbowl" activity as a way to discuss course topics
9:15	Guest lecturer: "Teaching and Learning through Writing"
10:15	Small group brainstorming on possible writing assignments
10:45	Break and group presentation set-up
11:00	GROUP PRESENTATIONS
12:00	Lunch (on your own)
1:30	Guest speaker: "Service Learning and Its Role in Student Success"
2:15	Mini-lectures and activities demonstrating
	• money management
	• academic integrity
	• academic advising/selecting a major/career development
2:45	Break
3:00	Guest speaker: "Connecting with International Studies"
3:10	Rituals and history of academe and of our institution
3:55	Acknowledge that tomorrow is last day—begin closure language
4:00	Dismiss

Assignment:
Begin developing a syllabus for your course; draft due tomorrow

Friday (Goals: Provide time for building a syllabus; evaluate the workshop; provide closure for community and individuals; review what has been accomplished; share tradition of "course song")

8:45	Gathering with coffee and refreshments
9:00	Review/preview
9:05	Course content and syllabus development
11:00	Workshop evaluation
11:30	Closure activities
	• hot seat
	• slide show of week's activities/participants
	• student success course song (each training group writes and adds a new verse)
12:30	Good-byes and lunch on your own

In addition to preparing new faculty to teach the course for the first time, it is important to consider how you will renew the commitment of continuing faculty as well as provide them with updated information about resources available for achieving course outcomes. One way is to have a daylong workshop or extended faculty meeting prior to the start of the semester. You might consider making this a more inclusive gathering of individuals who are interested in teaching the course in the future or who are teaching the same students in the context of their departmental courses. In this way, the student success course becomes a faculty development resource for the entire campus and can begin to influence the dialogue about student learning.

Following is an example of what such a workshop might look like.

A Daylong Workshop for Faculty Teaching Freshmen
Agenda

8:30–9:00 A.M. ....Gathering, Continental Breakfast

9:00 A.M. ....Welcome
Dr. Stanley Aeschleman, Provost, Senior Vice Chancellor of Academic Affairs

9:15 A.M. ....Plenary Session
Our featured presenter, John O'Connor of George Mason University, will speak about connections between Learning Communities, Freshman Seminar, and new learning technologies.

10:15 A.M. ....Break
Please use this opportunity to view the poster displays and Freshman Seminar resource table located in the hallway.

10:30 A.M. ....Learning Communities and Advising
Joni Petschauer will share information on Learning Communities and the new role academic advisors will play in Freshman Seminar.

11:00 A.M. ....Announcements and Campus Resource Opportunities
Guest speakers will share information about campus resources available to instructors. We will hear from representatives of the Office of Student Development (Cindy Wallace), Equity Office (Susan King and Amy Hathcock), and Health Services (Susan Tumbleston).

12:00 P.M. ....Lunch
Your table number is located on your name tag. Learning Community teams will be grouped together to encourage processing and semester planning.

1:30–2:30 P.M. & 2:45 –3:45 P.M. ....Concurrent Sessions
There will be a fifteen-minute break between sessions during which the poster displays will be repeated and refreshments will be available.

1:30–2:30 P.M. & 2:45–3:45 P.M.

4:00 P.M. ....Closing Session
> *We will spend a few minutes wrapping up the day, taking questions and comments, processing, and previewing the semester.*

Engaging Students–Promising Practices

Great emphasis is being placed on a number of practices that more fully engage students, faculty, and campus resources in the academic purposes of the campus community. None is more pervasive than the notion of outcomes-based education. This course provides an opportunity to teach students and faculty about the ability to demonstrate what they know through tangible projects, products and participation. Among these are learning communities, undergraduate research, service-learning, internationalizing the campus/curriculum, and summer reading/common book programs. These efforts immerse students, faculty, and staff in a collaborative process that focuses on the discovery and application of knowledge. They provide a hands-on context for a variety of contents and assessment indicates that student learning is enhanced and campus culture improved. But these ideas cannot be implemented without a strong faculty/staff development component. Consider the following examples as you develop campus connections that serve student success.

Learning Communities

In building a case for the development of learning communities on your campus, it is useful to consider what you want from each learning community partner, particularly the faculty and administrators who will support the effort. Faculty development should outline the expectations and contributions that are needed to implement and sustain the effort. Among the reasons that faculty will be motivated to participate in freshman level learning communities is an opportunity to connect earlier with students who might be interested in a specific major or field of study. Other faculty will be interested because of the interdisciplinary experiences and collaborative settings that are implied. It is important for your faculty development model to challenge faculty to make these connections and provide them with the support for it to happen.

Example of Two-Day Workshop for Faculty and Academic Support Team Members involved in a Learning Community

First Day

12:45–1:00 P.M.	Gathering and refreshments
1:00–1:30 P.M.	Welcome and overview of Freshman Learning Communities (FLC)
1:30–2:00 P.M.	Introduction of each FLC and the team member
2:00–2:45 P.M.	Brainstorming Session (in FLC teams) and report out
	What is a learning community? What sustains it?
2:45–3:00 P.M.	Break
3:00–3:15 P.M.	National conversation about learning communities
3:15–3:30 P.M.	The Campus Context for learning communities
3:30–3:45 P.M.	Assessment results
3:55–4:00 P.M.	Thank everyone for being there and prepare for tomorrow

Second Day

9:00–9:05 A.M.	Review yesterday's essential findings about learning communities
9:05–9:30 A.M.	Nuts and bolts: What do we have to offer the FLCs?

- Budget resources
- RAs; tutors; librarians; peer mentors
- Assessment and Program Evaluation
- Monthly team meetings: communication and expectations

9:30–11:15 A.M.   Brainstorming time for FLC teams
Specific tasks:

- consider unifying themes
- identify two to three specific activities/assignments that can be done that require input from each team member to contribute to the FLC; members to meet and discuss what they might use the FLC format to accomplish (guest speakers, field trips, group advising, community building, etc.). (Make certain that all support team members understand that the faculty determines the course syllabus)

Take your break

11:15–12:00 P.M.	Share ideas from each session
12:00–1:00 P.M	Lunch
1:00–3:00 P.M	Teaching groups through cross-disciplinary content
3:00–3:30 P.M	What? So what? Now what?

Undergraduate Research

The area of undergraduate research is probably one in which your faculty will not need a tremendous amount of guidance but it is always useful to gather individuals together and share your expectations for the work they choose to undertake. You might consider a series of workshops or informal conversations that place this work in the context of the institution's goals and to inform faculty of the resources available to them. Student-faculty mentoring relationships are important to foster but should be done with the student's well being and learning in mind. Below is an example of a workshop with general topics to consider.

Undergraduate Research–Faculty Workshop

12:00–1:15 P.M.	Lunch and overview of undergraduate research
1:30–4:40 P.M	Concurrent sessions (Topics: Four points of mentorship; Legal Implications of Undergraduate Research; Advisor/Advisee Relationship)
4:30–5:30 P.M	Campus resources: Library, Student Union, Media Services
5:30–6:00 P.M	Wine and Cheese Social

Service Learning

Many faculty members, like students, are naturally drawn to the service-learning pedagogy. Yet experienced faculty members who have utilized service learning in their courses encourage others to consider the time and training needed to do it well. Finding activities in the community that are already tied to course content is a crucial first step. Preparing students to be self-directed is an essential step before the co-curricular activity can take shape. And structured reflection must be a part of all service-learning courses. Many campuses offer support for training through a faculty development center or student development office. Workshops, stipends, conferences, and mentoring are all support mechanisms that will help grow service-learning programs on your campus. The following is an example of a semester-long workshop series for preparing faculty to engage in service-learning course work.

Service-Learning Workshop Series Agenda

The following series of workshops are designed to help new service-learning faculty members become acquainted with all aspects of this innovative and powerful pedagogy. *Sessions will be held from 3:30–5:30 P.M on the following Tuesdays:*

Sept 13: "Service-Learning 101" Facilitator: Shari Galiardi

Sept 27: "Advice From Veteran Faculty" (Panel Discussion) Facilitator: Dr. Betsy Beaulieu
Oct 4: "Developing Service-Learning Syllabi & Effective Reflection Assignments" Facilitator: Dr. Norm Clark

Oct 18: "Scholarship in Service Learning" Facilitator: Dr. Lynne Bercaw

Nov 1: "A Developmental Balancing Act: Intersections Between Student Development Theory & Service Learning" Facilitator: Shari Galiardi

Nov 15: "Working with Community Partners" (Panel Discussion) Facilitator: Todd Mortensen

Nov 29: Wine & Cheese "Graduation Party" for Faculty Fellow Participants (Deans, Department Chairs, Provost, and the Chancellor Will Be Invited to Attend)

Internationalizing the Campus/Curriculum

Scholarly travel, leading study abroad programs, and hosting international faculty are unique benefits afforded to many university faculty members. In terms of faculty development, these are coveted opportunities. Cultivating an interest in your student population regarding diversity, internationalization, and multicultural experiences should begin during the freshman year. Freshman Seminar is a natural place to start this conversation and faculty are good partners to share their experiences. One of the most important reasons to focus on internationalization is that students who experience broad and diverse opinions and people are more readily able to integrate complex experiences into their understanding of the world. If appreciation for difference matters, it is useful to provide faculty with tools to engage their students in honestly talking about how these differences create discomfort for them. In addition to preparing faculty to cope with logistical planning, communication support, and campus legal policies, it is important to address student development and integrative learning models. You want to ensure that students will be able to navigate a new culture appropriately (basic requests in the language and simple points of etiquette) if traveling abroad is involved. If the primary tool for internationalizing is course work on your own campus, bringing in multicultural specialists and activities can encourage active engagement.

Summer Reading/Common Book Programs

The faculty development process for a Summer Book Program can be as simple as a one-time workshop for faculty who wish to lead a discussion about the book or as complex as a year-long discussion linking the book to specific course and core curriculum outcomes. Whatever you choose to do, be aware that many publishers are willing to support these popular educational programs and have Web sites and study questions that support the use of books on college campuses. A faculty committee that is responsible for the text selection and faculty development workshops will embrace an opportunity to discuss a book.

McGraw-Hill Sponsored Faculty Development Workshops

Finally, McGraw-Hill Higher Education recognizes the value of preparing faculty to teach the concepts and ideas that are embodied in *P.O.W.E.R. Learning*. They are flexible and able to provide a range of workshops and speakers to meet the needs of groups of campuses seeking to improve the success of students and ability of faculty to deliver a high quality experience. To this end, they have generated a variety of workshop models that you might wish to explore with your campus representative. For more information on McGraw-Hill's Faculty Development Workshops and co-hosting opportunities contact your McGraw-Hill representative. They will be glad to assist you in accomplishing your goals. Following are examples of recent workshops sponsored in part by McGraw-Hill.

McGraw-Hill and Georgia Tech
Faculty Development Workshop
"Best Practices Equal Increased Retention"
****

8:30   Breakfast

9:00   Opening and Welcome
     Lisa Berry
     Field Publisher for Student Success, McGraw-Hill Publishing

     Dr. William Schafer
     Vice President for Student Affairs, Georgia Tech

9:15   Panel Discussion on Best Practices
     Dr. Keisha Hoerrner, Director of CLASS
     University Studies, Kennesaw State University

     Dr. Carolyn Codamo, Faculty Associate
     Office of Undergraduate Studies, Georgia State University

     Dr. Andrea Trinklein
     Director of Residence Life, Emory University

10:00 Move to Table Discussions with Panelists

12:00–1:30
     Lunch in the Student Center Commons

1:30   Keynote: "Student Success Practices that Improve Retention"
Joni Webb Petschauer, Appalachian State University

McGraw-Hill and Old Dominion University
Faculty Development Workshop
Friday, March 11, 2005

"Student Success and Learning Communities:
A Natural Connection"
Plus a Bonus Session!
"Student Success Courses: The Online Option"

9:00 to 9:30   **Welcome and Introductions**
Leslie Oberhuber
Marketing Manager for Student Success
McGraw-Hill Publishing

Dr. Dana Burnett, Vice President for Student Services & Dean of Students
Old Dominion University

9:30 to 12:00   **Student Success and Learning Communities:**
A Natural Connection, Part 1
Cindy Wallace, Appalachian State University

12:00 to 1:30   **Lunch Hosted by McGraw-Hill Publishing**

1:30 to 2:30   **Student Success and Learning Communities:**
A Natural Connection, Part 2
Cindy Wallace, Appalachian State University

2:30 to 3:30   **Student Success Courses: The Online Option**
Dr. Robert Feldman, University of Massachusetts–Amherst

3:30 to 4:00   **Q&A and Wrap Up**

One of the most ambitious activities sponsored by McGraw-Hill has been the Institute for Student Success and Academic Change (ISSAC), which is a partnership between Appalachian and McGraw-Hill Higher Education. This residential institute allows campuses to send teams to Appalachian in order to work on a campus-defined problem regarding student success. Below is an example of an institute schedule.

ISSAC	Arrival–Sunday 11/17	Day 1–Monday 11/18	Day 2–Tuesday 11/19	Day 3–Wednesday 11/20
EARLY MORNING		BREAKFAST 8–9 A.M. Broyhill Room	BREAKFAST ON YOUR OWN	BREAKFAST 8–9 A.M. Bernhardt Room
MORNING		9 A.M. KEYNOTE: Issues of Recruitment in Education – Joe Watts and Dr. Bobby Kanoy (XAP and UNC General Administration) Broyhill Room	9 A.M. KEYNOTE: Issues of Educational Access– Dr. Margarita Benitez (U.S. Department of Education) Broyhill Room	9 A.M. "NEXT STEPS" PANEL: Ms. Tina Milano (Exec. Dir. National College Access Network); Dr. Robert Feldman (Prof. of Psychology and Director of Undergraduate Studies at UMass, Amherst); Dr. Charles Duke (Dean of College of Education)
LATE MORNING		10:30–12:00 GROUP DISCUSSIONS: RECRUITMENT	10:30–12:00 GROUP DISCUSSIONS: ACCESS	10:30–11:00 CLOSURE AND EVALUATION
		LUNCH 12:15–2:00 P.M. KEYNOTE: Issues of Retention – Dr. Betsy Barefoot (Policy Center on the First Year of College) Luncheon sponsored by UNC General Administration	LUNCH and KEYNOTE 12–2:00 P.M.: Assessment – Dr. Randy Swing (Policy Center on the First Year of College) Broyhill Room	
EARLY AFTERNOON	1:00–3:00 P.M. Team Arrival; Registration	2:15–3:30 P.M.: GROUP DISCUSSIONS: RETENTION	2:15–5:00 P.M.: TEAM FUTURE THINK and PLANNING SESSION	
LATE AFTERNOON	3:00–5:00 P.M. Campus Tour and Orientation	3:30–5:00 P.M. Appalachian Places and Practices (Admissions, LAP, AAC, GEAR UP, Upward Bound, SSS, etc.)		
EVENING	6:00–8:00 P.M. Reception/Dinner at Appalachian House	DINNER ON YOUR OWN— Teams meet and debrief on their own		
			6:30–9:00 P.M. Celebration Dinner	

Implications for Broader Faculty Development on Your Campus - 67

IV

TEACHING THE TEXT: CHAPTER-BY-CHAPTER NOTES

Chapter 1

P.O.W.E.R. Learning: Becoming an Expert Student

I.   CHAPTER SUMMARY

Learning outcomes for this chapter

LO 1.1	Discuss the benefits of a college education
LO 1.2	Identify the basic principles of P.O.W.E.R. Learning
LO 1.3	Explain how expert students use P.O.W.E.R. Learning
LO 1.4	Compare and contrast learning styles and identify your own

Message to the student

       Starting off on the right foot is crucial. You are creating the foundation on which your academic career will depend. Make this foundation strong and broad enough to support a diverse and demanding college experience as well as establish a process you will use throughout your life. Be especially mindful that there are greater expectations of a person who has received a college education. You will be looked to for leadership in your work. You will be sought out to facilitate difficult conversations. You will be considered the change agent in your community.

       Learning is a personal journey. How you process information and what you choose to spend time learning is based on individual preferences and past experiences. A successful learner will learn "because of and in spite of" the teaching styles of instructors, the physical environment, or other circumstances. The more you know about yourself–strengths and weaknesses–the more you can strategically go about the process of becoming a better person. Your self-esteem will grow as you come to trust yourself as a confident and competent learner who can successfully negotiate diverse classrooms and instructors. This flexibility is a vital skill for navigating through the even more complicated world that awaits you beyond college. Embrace all of these expectations and challenges as you engage in your education.

Message to the instructor

       We invite you to explore these lessons with your students. Answer the questions provided by each chapter from your unique perspective as course facilitator. The P.O.W.E.R. Learning process outlined by Bob Feldman can enhance the skills and knowledge you already bring to the classroom experience. Learning to teach can be as tough as learning to learn.

       Chapter 1 encourages students to assess their strengths and weaknesses particularly as these characteristics influence success in the academic environment. Additionally, learning styles are covered in this chapter. Students are often fascinated by this information because it validates their individuality. Do not miss the opportunity to link different learning styles to different teaching styles. The concept of P.O.W.E.R. Learning is defined, and the process is outlined. Encourage your students to make a commitment to use this process now. Re-emphasize the P.O.W.E.R. plan each time you teach a chapter. By mid-term, you will find that your students use the process with ease.

       In addition to these fundamental ideas, we believe that the first days of class are vital for you to *begin* establishing the following ideas within your class:

- your role as the instructor.
- your expectations of your students.

- your students' expectations of the class and you.
- an awareness of the role of each student within the academic community.

And so begins your academic journey with your students. Use each day to assist your students become not only good citizens of your campus and classroom, but also of the world.

II. IDEAS AND CONCEPTS TO CONSIDER
Refer also to key terms listed in back of chapter.

civic engagement
civility
critical thinking
expert student
fear of success
goal setting
intellectual organization
LASSI
left-brain/right-brain processing
learning style or learning preferences
mental organization
motivation
Myers-Briggs Type Indicator
personal mission statement
personality style
physical organization
P.O.W.E.R Learning
self-assessment

III. CLARIFYING QUESTIONS AND DISCUSSION PROMPTS
At the end of each chapter in the Annotated Instructor's Edition (AIE), teaching tips, discussion prompts, student alerts and additional exercises and activities are organized around specific learning outcomes. These questions can be used to encourage class discussion, small group work, and/or individual reflection about the information presented in this chapter.

1. What do you want for your future and how does college support these plans?
2. What do you already know about yourself, especially how you learn, that can help you obtain your goals?
3. What do you know about yourself that will hinder you in obtaining your goals?
4. What do you look for in teachers? In classes?
5. What example of success and failure do you have with academic goals?
6. Who is in your life that can help you be academically successful?
7. How will being successful in your program affect your self-esteem?
8. What is P.O.W.E.R. Learning?
9. How can your college experience help you understand the world today as well as prepare you to deal with changes in the world in the future?

IV. CLASSROOM ACTIVITIES AND ASSIGNMENTS

Consider using the following exercises when teaching this chapter. Always refer to the Instructor's Annotations at the end of each chapter in the AIE. Those listed below with an asterisk (*) can be found at the end of this chapter in Section VIII; those with a double asterisk (**) are in the student text. Others are self-explanatory.

*Eating together–meal, coffee, etc. (20 minutes to 2 hours, in or out of class)
*Boundary Breaking (45 minutes to 1 hour, in class)
*Admit Cards (5 to10 minutes, out of class)
*Group Interaction Courses/Low Ropes Initiatives (3 to 4 hours, out of class)
**Journal Writing, Reflection Cards and Reaction Cards (10 to 20 minutes, in or out of class); see also AIE
*Forced Choice (20 to 40 minutes, in class); see also AIE
*LASSI (45 minutes, in or out of class)—this is a good time to explore the online resources (**www.mhhe.com/power**) particularly if you are teaching in a Smart classroom or if your students could bring laptops to class.
*The Learning Pyramid (20 to 30 minutes, in class)
*Myers-Briggs Type Inventory or other learning styles inventory (two class periods—one to administer the inventory and one to process the results). This may seem like a like a lot of time to devote to this information but it is extremely important to your students. And while you may not be an expert on learning styles, do not short shrift this chapter—become a learner.
*Introducing Preferences exercises (3 to 4 minutes, in class)

V. USING THE P.O.W.E.R. LEARNING PROCESS IN YOUR INSTRUCTION

Whether you are learning to learn or learning to teach, the P.O.W.E.R. Learning process is a useful tool. Here are our ideas for applying this process as an instructor with this chapter.

P.repare: Arrive in the classroom 15 minutes early. Make certain the room is arranged properly and is clean. Create a welcoming tone by writing your name on the board. Have nameplates available (we cut the ends of old file folders to create name tents). Bring a magic marker for writing names on the nameplates. Greet students as they enter. Establish through these actions that "being prepared and on time" is valued.

O.rganize: Decide one or two questions you wish students to consider today. Have a Boundary Breaking exercise available to use during the second or third class. (The first day is not the day to do this activity if students still have the option to drop or add the course.)

W.ork: During class have students *write, speak, and listen.* These skills are critical to learning. You can ask them to write a response to one question. They can then share their answer with an individual, a small group, or the whole class. In order to encourage listening, you should revise their original answers to reflect at least one other piece of information they have heard.

E.valuate: Ask students to write or say one thing they learned or share an unanswered question that they have at the end of class. Use this information to understand whether you were successful in getting your point across. Jot down on your syllabus whether you allotted enough time for all that you covered. Give yourself a grade for your effectiveness that day as the instructor. Acknowledge what you believe was on target.

R.ethink: Use the information and the experience to improve your teaching the next time you meet with the class; shorten the lecture, consider the interests of your students, allow for new directions.

TRY IT! In the space below, begin a teaching journal. In this jot down the ideas that worked and changes you would make the next time you teach this topic.

_____

_____

_____

_____

_____

_____

_____

_____

VI. CONNECTIONS WITHIN THE TEXT
This section is to remind you that a successful first year experience instructor must be a master weaver. The process of creating an intricate basket or an exquisite tapestry is the same process you must use in each class. Pull one lesson from the first week of class, one comment from a student mid-way through the semester, one journal entry from the second, anxiety-filled class day, and wisdom from the text–page linking page, chapter linking chapter. Weave the thoughts, words, reflections, and activities together; pull each thread, weave a garment, connect your students and this class to you and one another.

VII. CONTINUING THE CONVERSATION BEYOND THE CLASSROOM
Creating opportunities for learners to become actively involved in the process of thinking, doing, and reflecting is a key role for the instructor. During the first days of class, in addition to supporting the private dialogue between the textbook author and your students, you need to encourage students to share their thoughts with one another

and with you, thus extending the conversation into the classroom setting. We believe that you must consciously connect the course content to

- the individual student's life,
- the programs and practices in the broader academic community,
- the world in which we live–our global society.

Here are some ideas that can carry the conversation beyond the chapter activities.

GOAL: To connect the information to the individual student's life.

1. Request students to write a reflection card (3 to 5 sentences) that is turned in at the beginning of each class, focusing on a single question such as "What have I observed or accomplished about my educational goals since the last class?" These cards are often called *admit cards* and can be used to create a dialogue between the instructor and the student. Additionally, they can be used to check attendance, thus saving class time for discussion.

2. Personal relationships can take on a different texture when students consider how learning preferences influence choices and priorities. Ask students to reflect on a misunderstanding or conflict with a family member, friend, or colleague at work. Does the information on learning styles provide any insight to that situation?

GOAL: To connect the information to the programs and practices in the broader academic community.

1. Give students 10 to 15 index cards and ask them to list the skills needed to be successful in college (1 skill per card). Ask them to consider their courses, family life, work, and community obligations. After a period of about five minutes invite them to leave their desks and stand in a circle. Ask one student to state one of his or her skills and put the card with that skill on the floor; ask other students who have cards with the same or a similar skill listed to add their cards to the pile. Continue through until all cards have been placed in specific piles. Usually the cards can be divided into 10 to 15 different piles. This activity allows students to think and write as well as analyze and regroup their ideas. Furthermore, by having them leave their desks, you create valuable movement that keeps students physically and mentally involved in their work.

2. Ask your students to create an imaginary study group for a test either in your class or another subject. Given their knowledge about learning and teaching styles, what abilities need to be present in such a group for it to be successful? What would guarantee that the group would fail?

GOAL: To connect to the global society.

1. One of the greatest outcomes of a student success course is the communication that you encourage among your students. Several issues must be considered as you invite open discussion among your students and yourself. It is important to

create a trust-filled environment that allows for respectful and thoughtful listening to genuine and truthful responses. These skills are needed not only in the classroom, but in all civil interaction. One of the best activities we know of is called Boundary Breaking. It is useful for setting the stage for your students to understand how to share personal information and how to respond appropriately.

2. Learning preferences can be influenced both by culture and gender. Ask your students to compare the classroom experience of an American student with that of a Japanese student (or other non-Western group). How is the room set up? How long do they meet? How is information delivered? What is the level of participation by the students?

VIII. CLASSROOM ACTIVITIES TO SUPPORT TEACHING THIS CHAPTER
- Boundary Breaking
- Admit/Exit Cards
- Group Interaction Courses/Low Ropes Initiatives
- Journal Writing, Reflection Cards, and Reaction Cards; see also, AIE
- Forced Choice activity; see also, AIE
- Learning Pyramid
- Myers-Briggs Type Indicator
- Introducing Preferences

BOUNDARY BREAKING

One of the most important steps to building community is to encourage individuals to listen to one another. Most individuals are hesitant to share personal information upon first meeting in a group. This response is not only natural but also prudent. It is wise to be thoughtful about what and how much to reveal until a certain level of trust has been reached.

Over time, most classes often develop a sense of community but sometimes it is critical to accelerate this process in order to promote academic success. This exercise speeds up the process of students and faculty becoming aware of one another because the questions promote more than a superficial conversation.

Listening is basic to learning. Boundary Breaking practices and reinforces this skill. Past students and faculty have reported that the questions provoke thought and encourage personal sharing without becoming too personal for sharing with peers and teachers.

Facilitation

The teacher works best as the leader of this exercise. It is important that the teacher participate fully in the experience.

Time

Plan to do this exercise early in the semester; the second class period is generally best. Plan for this activity to last 45 minutes to 1 hour.

Setting

All persons should be in view of all group members. A circle works best. Sitting in desks is okay but the informality of setting on the floor works very well. (Should a participant have a physical disability that prevents him/her from sitting on the floor, have everyone sit at the disabled person's level.)

Close the classroom door to create a sense of privacy. Form the circle as tightly as possible. It is not recommended to do this activity outdoors because the sense of privacy may be lost, and answers may be more difficult to hear.

Nametags that are large enough to read from each point in the circle are strongly recommended.

Group Size

This exercise works best when everyone in the class participates together. Ideally, student success classes are 20 or fewer students. Experience shows that it can work with as many as 25 students before considering breaking the class into two smaller groups.

Special Instructions to the Leader

Placing name cards in front of participants helps people learn names. The teacher must present a serious face in introducing and conducting Boundary Breaking. Be especially careful of side conversations and jokes. Don't be afraid to share information about yourself.

It is important that the teacher encourage students to give honest answers, to express sincere feelings, and to respect the thoughts and feelings of others. One joker will ruin this experience for all. Laughs, and funny answers (when truthful and sincere) are delightful and natural expressions. These can also be defense mechanisms that hide us from others.

DO NOT EXPLAIN THE QUESTIONS. SIMPLY READ THE QUESTION AGAIN IF ASKED FOR AN EXPLANATION.

It is important for students to interpret the question and not for you to it for them. (This sets the tone for good teaching as well because it encourages students to see how there can be more than one "right answer" to a question.)
Ask students who speak softy to repeat their answer so all can hear.

Read these instructions to participants:

…Each person is to answer all questions.
…You may pass while you think, but we will always come back to you. (Leader may wish to appoint a helper who keeps track of people who pass.)
…No one is allowed not to answer.
…"I don't know" is not an answer.
…We are here to listen.
…We are not here to debate.
…We are not here to disagree.

…You may not comment on the answers of others or ask for explanations until the end.
…The key word is "listen"… "listen"… "listen."
…I will read a question, and the person to my right will answer, then the next person and the next… until everyone has answered the question. I will then read another question and the second person to my right will begin. Everyone will have the opportunity to answer first.
…Don't repeat the answers of others unless it is truly what you wished to say. (If students say "same as him/her," ask them to state the answer in their own words.)
…You may give any answer you wish, but answers must be honest and truthful. I request your sincere thoughts and feelings.

BOUNDARY BREAKING QUESTIONS
(May Be Presented in Any Order)

1. What is your favorite "toy" at this point in your life?
2. What is the title of the last book that you read?
3. What leisure time activity pleases you most?
4. What is the ugliest thing you know?
5. What is the greatest problem in the United States today?
6. What is the best regular program on television?
7. If you could smash one thing and only one thing, what would you smash?
8. If you could travel to any place in the world, where would you go first?
9. What emotion is strongest in you?
10. What do you think people like in you the most?
11. What do you think people like in you the least?
12. Who has most influenced your life?
13. What would you like to be talented at that you are not at the present time?
14. What TV advertisement bothers you the most?
15. What color is love … if you had to paint love?
16. What one day in your life would you like to live over?
17. What delights you most about being at _____[name of your institution]?
18. What is your strongest fear about being a college student?
19. If you were shipwrecked on a desert island, what one item would you most want to take? (You cannot take electronic entertainment or devices, e.g., radio, cell phone, TV, or a friend.)
20. If you could have a dinner conversation with anyone alive, who would it be?
21. If you could build one thing, what would you build?

SYNTHESIS SET

Instructions: Answer the next questions as you think about this exercise.

1. What answer (yours or someone else's) surprised you most?

2. The answer I want to know more about is _____.

3.   This group _____[complete the sentence].

4.   I promise this group _____[complete the sentence].

5.   Now, I feel _____[complete the sentence].

The leader should thank the group as an ending to this exercise. Groups often physically relax during the activity and the leader might note the success of the experience by calling attention to body positions. Invite people to ask questions, to continue conversations with someone they would like to know better, and so on as the class ends.

ADMIT/EXIT CARDS

There are many variations on this idea. Consider which of these ideas appeal to you; mix and match ideas or create your own. Here are some examples:

1. To be admitted to class, students are told ahead of time that they must arrive with a question about the topic to be discussed that day. The teacher arrives early and collects the card with the question at the door. No card, no admittance.
2. In the syllabus, students are informed that they must write a 3 to 5 sentence paragraph responding to the prompt "Since the last class, I have observed or accomplished the following about my educational goals…." The card with this paragraph is due at the beginning of each class period and must include the student's name and the date. Not only does this promote reflective thinking about learning but also it creates a private conversation between the faculty member and the student. Furthermore, the faculty member can use the cards to determine class attendance and when the cards are returned, the student has a record of his/her attendance as well.
3. Students are requested to record what they have read since the last class (be it required or for pleasure) and to provide comments about their readings. Placed on a 3×5 card, with the student's name and date, this card is taken up at the beginning of each class.
4. At the end of each class, students have to provide a card in order to leave. Request your students to do one of the following:
   - write a summary of the day's lesson.
   - write one question that has been left unanswered about the day's topic.
   - make an observation about how today's lecture applies to another class.
   - define a keyword that summarizes the lesson.
   - critique the instructor's teaching.
   - critique the student's participation.
   - identify the "muddiest point" from the lecture.
   - suggest what the next class topic should or will be.

GROUP INTERACTION COURSES
AND LOW ROPES INITIATIVES

Group Interaction Courses (GIC) and Low Ropes Initiatives provide students and faculty with powerful, memorable, and valuable learning opportunities. Many institutions have access to outdoor/experiential education services. These events are scheduled outdoors in a setting that encourages reflection and risk taking. It is important to note that many of these team problem solving activities can be carried out in an indoor facility as well as outdoors. The most important aspect is to schedule a substantial block of time (generally 3 to 4 hours) away from the classroom, with everyone committed to staying until the end. If your class is part of a learning community, be certain to invite other faculty and academic support team members.

A primary goal of this activity is to make the connection between risk taking and success. Whether the risk is physical, emotional, or intellectual, each person must question and communicate his or her strengths and weaknesses in order to be successful. This conversation about success and failure needs to be facilitated by the outdoor/experiential education leader; as the teacher, you need to be a participant with your students. A series of activities such as the Blind Man's Walk, the Trust Fall, the Wall, and/or other events will prompt the discussion. While the level of physical risk is relatively minimal in such programs, the level of personal psychological risk can seem high. A good group facilitator will recognize and work through these concerns with your group.

It is extremely important to communicate your expectations with your outdoor/experiential education facilitator. It is entirely reasonable to request that the activities be selected to assist you with your classroom goals such as:

- learning each other's names better,
- building group communication skills,
- practicing problem-solving skills,
- promoting personal challenge,
- encouraging self and group responsibility,
- setting the tone for high academic expectations, etc.

LOGISTICS OVERVIEW

Here are a few administrative hints for a successful GIC or Low Ropes Initiative:

- Book a date–Make a tentative reservation and place it on the syllabus prior to the start of class or identify two to three possible dates for scheduling the event early in the term. Simply make attendance an expectation and don't hesitate to suggest that it is a required assignment (just like reading a chapter in the textbook).
- Rain or shine–Yes, it is more fun to play outside on a clear, warm, sunny day, but that isn't how life always is. As long as it is safe (no lightning), your class can have an extremely positive and memorable GIC experience even if it is raining. Ponchos or other rain gear work quite well in the woods or wherever the course is. The facilitator has the expertise to make the judgment call about safety and should be allowed to do so.
- Meeting location–Have everyone gather at a specific location and bring your cell phone so that you can call students who are missing. Be sure to gather your students' cell phone numbers on the first day of class.

- Faculty involvement–You are encouraged to discuss your goals and expectations for the event with the GIC facilitator. Once the activities begin, the faculty member becomes just another member of the group. You should participate in all events, be careful not to "control" the group, and respect the authority of the GIC leader.

   Remember that many outdoor education programs use student leaders and so they are often still learning. They are trained and supervised, but minor difficulties can arise. If you are uncomfortable with the handling of the group or feel there is potential danger, you should make this known privately to the GIC leader.

   Should an emergency arise–sudden change in the weather, accident, and so on–the GIC leader will be responsible for taking control of the situation. You might be called upon to assist but you should fully support their leadership role and their practiced process.

- Cost–Most outdoor education programs charge a nominal fee for students to participate in this event.

- Follow-up to the event–Continue to refer to the GIC/Low Ropes Initiative throughout the semester. It is important to bring the experience into the classroom and to use this event as a reference point and metaphor for learning and self-challenge.

GIC/LOW ROPES INTIATIVES RESPONSE PAPER

Assignment Rationale

Many students report that the GIC/Low Ropes Initiative is one of the most powerful experiences they encounter as a community of learners. They tell us that the impact reaches far beyond the group challenges, class fun, and individual self-discovery. Specifically, they say that it raises questions about what college is about and what it can do for each individual. For the faculty member, it is a rare opportunity to spend a significant amount of time with students in a focused learning experience away from the classroom. Thus, we recommend that you take advantage of the powerful introspection that is begun by the activity.

   You will want to require that students attend the activity but you need to grade them on their ability to *process rather than just participate* in what happens. Thus, assigning a paper, presentation, or other project will be crucial. A wide range of important questions that center around issues such as those included in the following list might give you some ideas of how your students might process this experience:

- Building community
- Developing relationships with students and faculty
- Valuing differences
- Seeking assistance
- Recognizing and creating opportunities
- Following instructions
- Communicating effectively

- Planning
- Dealing with criticism and failure
- Cheating
- Focusing attention
- Managing time
- Knowing when to evaluate
- Understanding teamwork

- Knowing when to ask questions and negotiate
- Respecting the environment
- Stereotypes and gender issues
- Learning can be fun

There are certainly others but these few suggest the scope and power of this event as a learning experience for your students to consider.

Procedures
The goal of this project is to prepare a two- to three-page reflective paper summing up your experience. This will require three steps.

Step 1: Brainstorming
Pick 12 of the topics listed above (building community, following instructions, etc.) that seem to be the most important part of your GIC experience. Write each at the top of a 3 × 5 note card (you will create 12 cards). Spend two minutes for each card and note what you saw or learned related to that topic. Your notes may be a connection to the classroom, something about group behavior, or your personal feelings about how or why something worked or didn't work. (It can be a sentence, a couple of words, or a paragraph. The important point is to note your views.) NOTE CARDS ARE TO BE TURNED IN WITH THE FINAL PAPER.

Step 2: Organization
Next review your 12 note cards and try to organize them around natural themes. Your themes might include things like problem solving, trust, or whatever else emerged from your brainstorming.

Step 3: Writing
The final task is to write a two- to three-page reflective paper on your GIC experience. Using your three to four themes and note card observations, you should focus on what the GIC meant to you. Note in particular the connections between your experience on the GIC and the classroom.

Important Note: Papers should include an introduction that explains the purpose of the paper, a main body that develops and connects the separate themes, and a conclusion that sums up your main arguments. Papers will be evaluated on the basis of content, style, correct use of English, and following instructions.

JOURNAL WRITING, REFLECTION CARDS, AND REACTION CARDS

Processing personal experiences through written reflection is an important part of thinking and learning. Most student success course faculty use some form of written communication to keep in touch with students about events and self-discovery. These writings are a way to create a private conversation between you and your students and to assess the integration of experiences in your students' understanding of your course goals.

There are several factors to consider regarding these writings and there are a variety of ways to manage them. Here are a few examples:

- Semester long notebooks with multi-entries (usually weekly) that are evaluated quarterly
- End of class reaction cards where students spend the last five minutes summarizing the class and the impact or influence that specific information has on the student
- A sequence of papers guided by assigned topics and assembled in a portfolio
- Weekly reaction cards and e-mail entries that respond to self-discovery and goals

It is important that these be evaluated regularly and that personalized feedback is given to the students.

FORCED CHOICE

"Thinking on your feet" is a skill that is valued in many environments; the Forced Choice exercise allows this to happen naturally. Create a list of eight to ten statements or questions on any topic and label one end of the room as Agree and the other end as Disagree. Pose the statement or question and have the students move to the appropriate side of the room. Allow individuals to explain their choice without creating an opportunity for discussion. Then, quickly move on to the next question. This activity allows students to move around the room, to speak, and to listen.

LEARNING PYRAMID

The Learning Pyramid is a wonderful teaching/learning activity. Pair up the students and ask one person from each pair to volunteer to be the teacher–the other will be the learner. Ask each of the teachers to step outside of the room with you. Once outside of the room, you need to provide each of them with a copy of the Learning Pyramid (see below). The task of each teacher is to find a way to teach the information on the page without showing the sheet to the student or using the word *pyramid* to describe how the information is organized on the sheet. Give your teachers a full five minutes to study the information and determine their strategy for teaching it. You may choose to let them work on a similar strategy together or separately; there is merit in both approaches. During the five-minute preparation period, you may go back in the classroom and discuss something else with the students who are in the classroom. At the end of the preparation period, take up all copies of the pyramid and tell the teachers they have five minutes to teach the information to their students. Inform everyone that at the end of the teaching session, a test will be given to see if the students know the information. When the five minutes is up, ask everyone to recreate the information that was on the sheet. They should share their picture.

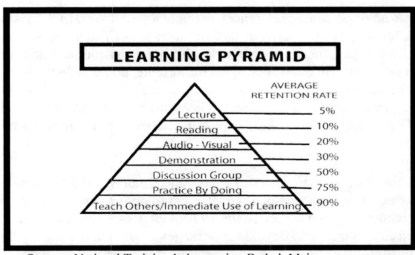

Source: National Training Laboratories, Bethel, Maine

Processing This Exercise

Ask everyone to answer the following question: Who was the learner, and who was the teacher? Why? What implication does this have for studying? For teaching? For learning?

MYERS-BRIGGS TYPE INDICATOR (MBTI) OVERVIEW

The MBTI is one of many assessment tools that can be used when discussing learning styles. It is among the most commonly used inventories of its kind because of its accessibility and ease of administration, the extensive research and documentation that accompanies its results, and its familiarity among educators. The MBTI is not a test with right or wrong answers but is an assessment of what individuals report as their preferences. It is important for your students to hear that your goal is not to stereotype or label them but rather assist them in understanding themselves. Below is a sample introduction and explanation for using the MBTI. Similar information can be developed about other learning inventories that you might choose to use.

Introduction

Have you ever wondered why you loved history and your classmate hated it? Have you ever felt inspired by one particular faculty member while your friends thought she was boring? Have you ever been uncomfortable at a party while others seem to be having a wonderful time? Do you ever wonder why some students miss deadlines and never seem to have things organized? All of these are connected to our personality type and our preferred way of doing and viewing the world.

Try this experiment. Hold your arms out. Bring them together and clasp your hands together. Look at which thumb is on top. Is it your right or left thumb? Now do the same thing, but this time change thumbs so that the other one is on top. It usually feels awkward, even uncomfortable. Do it again with your favorite thumb on top. If you clasped your hands together thousands of times you would probably place your favorite thumb on top every time because it is your *preference*.

We have the same kind of personal preferences in our learning styles. In a classroom environment that matches our learning style, everything feels right. The professor is stimulating, the material exciting, the work enjoyable. But if the environment does not match our preferred learning style, we feel out of place, uncomfortable, and unable to do our best.

There are no right or wrong, good or bad learning styles, just preferred styles. Understanding learning styles and personality preferences has helped students succeed in and out of class by providing an important dimension of self-discovery and personal growth.

Background

The MBTI developed out of the efforts by Isabel Myers and Katherine Briggs to understand the differences and similarities in human personalities. It is based on the psychological theory of Carl Jung, a Swiss psychologist, who argued in the 1920s that personality traits are inherited. Myers and Briggs used Jung's theory to develop four ranges of personality traits [Introvert-Extrovert (E-I), Sensing-Intuitive (S-N), Thinking-Feeling (T-F), Perceiving-Judging (P-J)] and numerous combinations. They refined their definitions over and over again during the 1940s and 50s by administering thousands of assessments. Today their personality assessment instrument is widely used by educators in the United States. It is not like other psychological tests in that it does not uncover illness or psychosis; it was designed to help normal people understand human behavior.

MBTI Definitions

What follows is a very abbreviated overview of the personality traits of the eight types developed by the Myers-Briggs Type Indicator. They are arranged in four continuums or scales:

1. Extrovert (E) ...... Introvert (I)
2. Sensing (S) ...... Intuitive (N)
3. Thinking (T) ...... Feeling (F)
4. Perceiving (P) ...... Judging (J)

We all have bits of each but tend to favor one end of the scale over the other. The stronger the number we score on the MBTI, the stronger our preference in that area. The lower our number, the more balanced the two preferences are.

Extrovert-Introvert: This scale explains how you get your energy.Extroverts (E) are energized by interaction with others. They love to talk, participate, organize, party. They are people of action. Extroverts are pulled into social life and find it difficult to settle down, read, or concentrate on homework. They hate to listen and need to talk to work out their ideas. They will find many college tasks challenging (reading, research, writing) because these are solitary endeavors.

Introverts (I) are energized by the inner world of reflection, thought, and contemplation. They need space and time alone. Introverts like reading, lectures, and written over oral work. They usually have a longer attention span and prefer to think things through before acting. Introverts are uncomfortable in discussion groups, may find it difficult to remember names, and hesitate to speak up in class. Introverts will have fun at a party if they can talk with one person all night.

Sensing-Intuitive: This scale suggests how you take in information. It has the biggest impact on how we learn. Sensing (S) people rely heavily on their five senses to take in information. They like concrete facts, organization, and structure. They are good at memorization, are usually realistic, and are relatively conventional. They are oriented toward the present, the concrete, and the here and now. Sensing people usually like clear guidelines and specifics. They often have difficulty with theory. They ask who, what, when, where. Sensing students read the question several times before answering it to be certain they understand it.

Intuitive (N) people see the world through intuition. They learn by hunches, look at the forest rather than the individual trees. They want to know the theory before deciding that facts are important. They are creative, innovative, and work with bursts of energy. Intuitives will write their term paper and then finish the required outline. Intuitives will always ask "why" before anything else. Intuitive students may not read a test question all the way through, sometimes missing a key part, because they act on their hunches.

Thinking-Feeling: This range tells how we like to make decisions. Thinking (T) people decide on the basis of logic, analysis, and reason. They follow their head rather than their heart, value truth over tact, and sometimes appear blunt and uncaring about the feelings of others. They usually have strongly held principles, value fairness over everything, and need purpose. People who must make decisions that negatively effect many individual lives (surgeons and corporation presidents) are often thinking types.

Feeling (F) persons follow their heart rather than their head. They decide on the basis of their feelings, personal likes and dislikes. They want others to like them so they find it difficult to say no or disagree with others. Feeling types need and value kindness. Feeling types value harmony and are distressed by interpersonal friction. Feeling types are often found in social work, elementary school teaching, and other helping professions. They feel rewarded when they can help others.

Judging-Perceiving: This range suggests the type of lifestyle and work habits we prefer. Judging (J) types try to order and control their world. They are decisive, may be close-minded, and are usually well organized. They meet deadlines, like planning, and prefer to work on only one thing at a time.

Perceiving (P) types are spontaneous and don't like to be boxed in by deadlines or plans. They want to gather more information before making a decision. They work at many things at once. Perceiving types are flexible and often good in emergencies when plans are disrupted. Their biggest problem is procrastination. They must make a calendar of things-to-do, but will probably lose it.

Conclusion
Myers-Briggs Type Indicators can help to explain some of the mysteries of college life. This information can be used in conjunction with learning, communication skills, developing successful relationships, choosing courses/majors/careers, working with others, and many other topics. Ultimately, the goal is to provide our students with information that can assist them in becoming more successful in the classroom and beyond.

INTRODUCING PREFERENCES

There are several ways to introduce students to the idea of learning preferences; most are simple and take very little time. A quick illustration is described in the overview of the Myers-Briggs Type Indicator. In that exercise, you ask your students to clasp their hands together. They should look and see which thumb is on top. Ask them to open their hands and re-clasp them, this time being certain to place the other thumb on top. All of your students will be able to successfully accomplish this but they are likely to say that it isn't comfortable or isn't natural. So it is with learning new ways of doing other things. Becoming aware of their existing learning preferences will empower students to understand why it sometimes is awkward or uncomfortable to learn differently than they did in previous learning environments. Perhaps the most important perspective to share with your students is that when the learning is tough, it doesn't necessarily mean that the student is stupid or the teacher can't teach ... just that they don't understand information in the same ways or possibly describe what they understand with the same words. Students who know about learning styles and preferences are simply better able to expand their repertoire skills than students who don't know about these ideas.

Chapter 2

Making the Most of Your Time

I.   CHAPTER SUMMARY
      Learning outcomes for this chapter
      LO 2.1   Explain how to manage time more effectively
      LO 2.2   Analyze how to deal with competing priorities
      LO 2.3   Identify strategies for dealing with surprises and distractions

      Message to the student
            This chapter provides an opportunity for the student to become aware of time
      management techniques and strategies that can influence not only academic success but
      also personal success. New technological devices have led to incessant interruptions in
      our lives. It takes self-discipline and self-understanding to know when it is appropriate
      to tune in and when you should tune out. Use this chapter to become aware of the time it
      takes for individuals (and yourself) to accomplish the tasks that you choose as priorities.

      Message to the instructor
            When work, family, and school collide, our students often feel like their lives
      reflect the Army's old television commercial—"we get more things done by 9 a.m. than
      most people get done all day." Invariably, this causes stress because of the unrealistic
      expectations of what can be done and what must be done. Students will arrive with a
      variety of time management skills and tools shaped by their lifestyle, habits, and
      attitudes. As with many behaviors, rather than trying to convince them that there are one
      or two right ways to manage time, a more useful opening question is to ask students if
      they are satisfied with the results of how they use their time. The focus should be on
      their engagement over time with tasks and activities that matter. If they are satisfied
      with the results of how the time is spent, then the likelihood or, even the need of,
      changing their behavior is low. If they are not satisfied with the results, then they might
      be more interested in learning ways to change. The ability to use time wisely might best
      be taught by your students. Assess through class discussion those students who are
      successful with their time and ask them to share strategies that work with those who
      want more information.

II.   KEY IDEAS AND CONCEPTS TO CONSIDER
      Refer also to key terms listed in back of the chapter.

      balance
      e-break
      priorities
      procrastination
      self-management
      visualization

III.   CLARIFYING QUESTIONS AND DISCUSSION PROMPTS
At the end of each chapter in the Annotated Instructor's Edition (AIE), teaching tips, discussion prompts, student alerts and additional exercises and activities are organized around specific learning outcomes. These questions can be used to encourage class discussion, small group work, and/or individual reflection about the information presented in this chapter.

1.   What tools are useful for getting the most out of your day or your time?
2.   When everything seems important, how do you determine what to do first?
3.   How long does it take for you to
      • read a chapter in a textbook?
      • read 20 pages in a novel?
      • review for a test in a course for which you are working for a "B"? an "A"?
      • eat a meal?
      • handle a routine task at work?
      • catch up with your family?
      • check your e-mail?
      • make a phone call?
      • sleep and feel rested?
4.   What time of day do you consider your prime time?
5.   What do you do during your prime times?
6.   What is one habit you could change regarding your use of time?
7.   What are your beliefs about time management?
8.   How will you use time management skills when you are at home or work?

IV.   CLASSROOM ACTIVITIES AND ASSIGNMENTS
Consider using the following exercises when teaching this chapter. Always refer to the Instructor's Annotations at the end of each chapter in the AIE. Those listed below with an asterisk (*) can be found at the end of this chapter in Section VIII; those with a double asterisk (**) are in the student text. Others are self-explanatory.

Use the calendar and all course syllabi to map out the semester; students can predict early on when the busy times will be (15-20 minutes, in or out of class)
* Planning Backwards (10-15 minutes, in or out of class)
* 168 Hours in a Week Check Sheet (in or out of class; 20 minutes); see also, AIE
* The Cost of Higher Education (15-20 minutes, in class)
** Try It! 2 (in class, 25 minutes total-10 minutes individual time, 15 minutes of group time)
** Try It! 4 (in class, 20 minutes total-5 minutes individual time, 15 minutes of group time)

V.   USING THE P.O.W.E.R. LEARNING PROCESS IN YOUR INSTRUCTION
Whether you are learning to learn or learning to teach, the P.O.W.E.R. Learning process is a useful tool. Here are our ideas for applying this process as an instructor with this chapter:

P.repare: Consider your attitudes and biases regarding time management. Ask yourself how this will affect your teaching this topic.
Make copies of the weekly time chart. Bring your own tools to class to show students: calendar, watch, things-to-do lists, smart phones, cell phones, and other electronic gizmos.

O.rganize: Allow for a follow-up day in your syllabus to discuss time management after students have begun using these skills.
Look at your lesson plan for time management. How is your style and preference reflected in the classroom?

W.ork: During class allow students to create a things-to-do list and a weekly plan; use the exercises in the text. Ask students to create a list of ways that they waste time or that they allow others to waste their time. Ask students to list ways they have successfully used their time. Ask them to describe their engagement in their learning–effectively using the time to learn.
What do they miss when they are not fully engaged? Give students a sample long-term assignment (i.e., ten-minute PowerPoint presentation that is due six weeks from today) and have them determine the tasks and time frame for accomplishing this assignment. As a class, discuss the different considerations for successfully completing this assignment.
Ask students to bring in their syllabi and calendars. Request that they write all of their tests and major assignments in their calendars. Do they notice that tests fall on similar weeks? Are there patterns for assignments? Does this information provide insight to when there will be stress periods during the semester? Can your students create strategies for dealing with this predictable stress?

E.valuate: One week after the initial discussion/lecture about time management, take another class period and ask for time schedules. Ask students to report their awareness of time wasters. Compare this information to the first discussion. Are your students more or less aware of how they use their time? How do they cope with the constant rings, beeps, and sounds that vie for their attention throughout the day?

R.ethink: Ask your students to consider how they will change the way they plan their use of time. An assignment to consider is requesting your students to review their calendar a month later and to see if they have changed their habits. Are they feeling less stressed out?

Are they able to develop human relationships that are based on face-to-face interaction and not solely through the assistance of technology? What role does face-to-face contact play in the educational experience? In the life of an educated person? These topics are particularly important to return to later in the semester as students come to understand that there is an ebb and flow to the work pace over a course term.

TRY IT!   In the space below, begin a teaching journal of the ideas that worked and changes you would make the next time you teach this topic.

_____

_____

_____

_____

_____

_____

_____

VI.   CONNECTIONS WITHIN THE TEXT
Consider bringing up this chapter's ideas again in the following contexts:

Chapter 1	a natural connection between goal setting and this information
Chapter 4	test taking connects nicely; particularly, planning time for test preparation
Chapter 5	reading requires time .... it is important to understand that good readers are flexible regarding reading speed based on the type of material they are reading
Chapter 6	time management is one of the most frequently connected "academic to job" skills
Chapter 10	stress management is greatly influenced by a student's use of time

VII.   CONTINUING THE CONVERSATION BEYOND THE CLASSROOM
Creating opportunities for learners to become actively involved in the process of thinking, doing, and reflecting is a key role for the instructor. In addition to supporting the private dialogue between the textbook author and the student, you need to encourage students to share their thoughts with one another and with you, thus extending the

conversation into the classroom setting. We believe that you must consciously connect the course content to

- the individual student's life,
- the broader academic community,
- the world in which we live—our global society.

Here are some ideas that can carry the conversation beyond the chapter activities:

GOAL: To connect the information to the individual student's life.

1. Ask your students to consider what they want to accomplish in the next five years. What kinds of relationships, jobs, skills, and talents do they want to have? Then ask them to work backwards and consider what they hope to accomplish within one year. Finally, ask them to make a list of the things they want to accomplish tomorrow. Do they see a correlation between tomorrow's tasks and their "hoped for" accomplishments at the end of the year? At the end of five years? The relationship between "the activities I participate in today and the abilities I have in the future" is fundamental for students to grasp. Have them write an intention or reflection statement about this idea.

GOAL: To connect the information to the programs and practices in the broader academic community.

1. Ask students to consider the organizations and extracurricular activities that are available and attractive to them. Can they identify skills or experiences that can be gained through membership to one of those groups? If so, they can see participation as both a benefit from an educational or career viewpoint. Often students will tell you that they would love to join a group or participate in volunteer project but that they do not have time. Remind them that the habits developed in school will be those they carry into their communities. Consider using the "168 hours in a day" check sheet to see how many "waking, uncommitted" hours they really have in a week. Student leaders indicate that development of strong self-management/time management skills provided them with the ability to take advantage of unique and life-changing opportunities.

GOAL: To connect to the global society.

1. The bulk of this chapter is focused on preparing a student to make the "most of their time" as it is valued in United States. Consider asking students to become more aware of how this is not the only way to view time. Make an assignment for your students to meet with an international student, a visiting faculty member from another country, or with an instructor who has taught abroad. Encourage them to find out how time is valued or used within the context of that culture. Specifically, ask your students to compare mealtime habits, phrases popular in the culture that refer to time (in the United States, we use phrases like "time is money," "24/7," and "time flies when you are having fun"). What differences or

similarities do they notice? What do they believe accounts for these differences? Ask them to write a paper or reaction card on this.

VIII.   CLASSROOM ACTIVITIES TO SUPPORT TEACHING THIS CHAPTER
- Planning Backwards
- 168 Hours in a Week; see also, AIE
- The Cost of Higher Education

PLANNING BACKWARDS

A good time manager keeps a daily to-do list, a weekly schedule, semester calendar, and regular assignment list. Yet these devices serve only to alert students (and others) of upcoming commitments; they do not keep assignments from being done at the last minute. The concept of "planning backwards" can help with this concern. You can illustrate this idea through the following case study:

> *Two weeks from today, Sarah must turn in an 8-10 page paper analyzing the differences between the Allied air attack on Germany in 1943-45 and the NATO air strikes against Yugoslavia in 1999. Her professor wants her paper to be double-spaced and printed rather than sent through e-mail. As part of her documentation, she needs to provide at least three Web sites that are accurate, accessible, and current as well as appropriate citations for any other materials that she uses. Naturally, she has several other assignments and commitments during this two-week period: attending 8 hours of class lectures, reading 60 pages in her history textbook during the next 3 days, daily math homework that takes about 2 hours each day, the open house at her 5th grade daughter's school, a planned trip home to visit her husband's parents over the weekend, and a full time job.*

Ask your students to take this situation and using a calendar, plan back from the due date, the steps and time it will take to complete the paper at least 24 hours before it is due. Tell them to put themselves in Sarah's shoes and to allot the time it would take them personally to complete each commitment. Hand out a two-week schedule and ask them to indicate on each day what will be done. You can have them share their solutions in small groups and/or you can provide feedback on their individual plans. This type of planning requires a self-awareness that is critical to student success. It is a habit to encourage and refer to throughout the semester.

168 HOURS IN A WEEK

This activity allows you to understand how you use your time each week. Everyone has the same amount of time and knowing how you choose to use your time will give you the power to change your behaviors.

Step 1. List the amount of time per week for each activity (arrive at a daily average and multiply by 7; account for weekend differences):
   a. Class time (# of hours in class each week)   _____
   b. Job/work   _____

c. Studying   _____

d. Commuting/transportation time   _____

e. Extracurricular activities (clubs, church, etc.)   _____

f. Family responsibilities (cleaning, cooking, shopping)   _____

g. Sleeping   _____

h. Eating   _____

i. Personal grooming (bathing, hair, make-up, etc.)   _____

Step 2: Add together "a-i" for a SUBTOTAL   =   _____

Now subtract your subtotal from 168 for a TOTAL =   _____

If the number in your TOTAL line is negative, you have committed more time than there is in a week. YOU ARE IN TROUBLE. If you have time left over, ask yourself what choices there are for your time. Do you have time for more sleep? Volunteering? Friends?

THE COST OF HIGHER EDUCATION

A simple way to enlighten students concerning the value of their money is by illustrating the cost of a college education. Use this activity to have students come up with the true investment they are making in college.

Procedure

Step 1.   Have students figure out how much it actually costs per year to attend school. Encourage them to add in all of the costs, even if there is not a category (such as belonging to a club or organization). They should determine what their total expenses would be throughout their entire educational program (one, two, four, five, or even six years).

Step 2.   Next, ask your students to do a Web search of starting salaries of two types of jobs: those requiring an undergraduate college degree and a typical job (usually minimum wage) that does not require an undergraduate degree. Multiply each salary type by 30 years of employment (just arrive at the gross number; do not try to adjust for raises, benefits, increase in minimum wage, inflation, or deductions for taxes, insurance, etc.)

Step 3.   Subtract the cost of an undergraduate education from the gross amount of working for 30 years in a job requiring such an education. Then compare that to the total amount earned if the student simply went to work and did not earn an undergraduate education.

Step 4.   Ask them what they have discovered. Are they making an investment in going to college? Are they likely to earn more over a lifetime with a college degree than without one? How much of an investment is their degree in their future financial security.

Chapter 3

Taking Notes

I.   CHAPTER SUMMARY
     Learning outcomes for this chapter

LO 3.1	Discuss what it means to take effective notes
LO 3.2	Explain methods for taking notes in class
LO 3.3	Explain methods for taking notes from written materials

Message to the student

    An active, engaged learner needs and wants to remember information. Often students believe that only when the teacher is talking is it necessary to take notes and sometimes not even then. Class discussions, multimedia presentations (and these are more sophisticated than ever!), student presentations, readings, and co-curricular activities are all appropriate times for taking notes. Often we associate note taking with classes but clubs, organizations, and offices always need individuals who possess this skill. Taking notes allows you to organize your thoughts about someone else's ideas. When reviewed, your notes provide you with an opportunity to question information in light of your own experiences. Finally, when done conscientiously, taking notes can provide you with a chance to create new knowledge.

Message to the instructor

    Students will not easily or openly embrace note taking as a habit or skill to develop. Students can tell you that they do not have good study skills but they will have a hard time changing their system. You will have to reinforce this information in order to get your point across—inspect their notes, treat the activity as an important step in the process of learning but try not to lose perspective about it. Note taking is an important skill but taking notes does not replace understanding information. Still, you want to encourage your students to be diligent and aware that the information shared in the college classroom is different than information shared in high school. To make this happen, you may need to be overly dramatic about its importance–exaggerate its ability to unlock the treasures of academe or solve the mysteries of our time. (This takes practice but it can be done!)

    Let students know that you are aware that after more than a decade of personalizing their own system for making the grade, a shift in taking notes will not come easily. This is especially true if your students are receiving the grades they want; under these circumstances there is little chance that they will change their habits. However, there are some skills that can make work easier and the time spent on it shorter—if we only had those skills and knew how to use them. An efficient, consistent note taking system is such an ability. If your class is part of a learning community, this is a great chapter for making connections between the courses. Your students can learn about note taking in your classroom and then practice the skill in the other classes. In addition, many institutions are now supplementing classroom instruction with a service learning component. This experience creates a real-world application of academic strategies such as note taking and may bring a relevance to the importance of these skills that the classroom does not provide.

Finally, consider your own willingness to write down information when people are speaking; consider role modeling good note taking by writing down information as your students speak.

II.   KEY IDEAS AND CONCEPTS TO CONSIDER
        Refer also to key terms listed in back of chapter.

        listening
        speaking
        key ideas
        meta-message
        concentration
        rethinking

III.   CLARIFYING QUESTIONS AND DISCUSSION PROMPTS
        At the end of each chapter in the Annotated Instructor's Edition (AIE), teaching tips, discussion prompts, student alerts and additional exercises and activities are organized around specific learning outcomes. These questions can be used to encourage class discussion, small group work, and/or individual reflection about the information presented in this chapter.

        The Journal Reflections "How Do I Take Notes?" is an excellent source of questions.

        1.   How would you evaluate your note taking ability?
        2.   What connection exists between note taking and academic success?
        3.   What do you do during class? How do you concentrate? How do you remember important information shared during class?
        4.   What do you look for in your notes when you are preparing for a test?
        5.   In what situations would a good note taking system prove useful outside of the academic environment?
        6.   What tools do you use and find helpful for taking notes?

IV.   CLASSROOM ACTIVITIES AND ASSIGNMENTS
        Consider using the following exercises when teaching this chapter. Always refer to the Instructor's Annotations at the end of each chapter in the AIE. Those listed below with an asterisk (*) can be found at the end of this chapter in Section VIII; those with a double asterisk (**) are in the student text. Others are self-explanatory.

        Evaluate a classmate's notes (20 minutes, in class); learning communities provide the best context for this activity
        *Admit/Exit Cards (5 to 10 minutes, out of class)
        *Using Films in the College Classroom (30 minutes, in class); see also AIE
        *1/4—3/4 Recall Method of Note Taking (30 minutes, in class)
        **TRY IT! 3 (40 minutes, in class)

**TRY IT! 4 (10 minutes, out of class)
**Course Connections—Asking questions from notes is a seemingly simple task that students might first ignore. Emphasize this behavior for success in class with constant practice.

V.   USING THE P.O.W.E.R. LEARNING PROCESS IN YOUR INSTRUCTION
Whether you are learning to learn or learning to teach, Bob Feldman's P.O.W.E.R. Learning process is a useful tool. Here are our ideas for applying this process as an instructor with this chapter.

P.repare: Assign your students to bring a week's worth of notes to class from another class. Also have them create a written observation of a model student in another class. In their observation, have them respond to the following questions:
- What tools did the model student bring to class?
- When did this student arrive to class?
- What did this person do during the class lecture?

OR
Ask the students to attend a lecture and take notes. Use this common experience to compare notes.

OR
If you are part of a learning community, go to the other class and take notes with your students. Use your notes to compare what was heard and written by your students.

OR
If your class has a service-learning requirement, have students take notes during every stage of the process as their relationship with their client develops. This can be a journaling exercise.

O.rganize: Identify a course in which all of your students will take notes to bring to your class; make the assignment two or three class periods prior to when you would like to cover note taking in your own course. Each individual must complete this assignment.

W.ork: With the notes in hand, have your students work in small groups to determine who has good notes. Create a list of characteristics that all of your students believe to be common in all good notes. If you are in a Smart classroom or have access to technology that allows you to do so, display the notes so that students can see who recorded what information.

E.valuate: The best way to evaluate the effectiveness of notes is after a test. Ask your students to write a brief evaluation of their success on a test in your class, or even better—in another class—based on the notes they took. What do they need to change about their note taking to be successful on future tests?

R.ethink: Revisit this information in two weeks. Ask your students to pair up and
               share their notes from another class again—are there differences? What
               shifts can they determine two weeks later? Four weeks later? Consider
               giving extra credit to a student who can illustrate a change in their note
               taking style based on a thoughtful re-evaluation of their earlier style.

TRY IT!   In the space below, begin a teaching journal of the ideas that worked
          and changes you would make the next time you teach this topic.

_____

_____

_____

_____

_____

VI.   CONNECTIONS WITHIN THE TEXT
      Consider bringing up this chapter's ideas again in the following contexts:

      Chapter 1   link note taking to their preferred learning/thinking styles
      Chapter 2   remind students that good note taking is a time saver for test
                     preparation
      Chapter 4   students rely on notes when preparing for tests
      Chapter 5   connect note taking to ways to be actively engaged when reading
                     and reinforce that writing information down makes it easier to
                     remember
      Chapter 6   if you want to remember what needs to be done on the job you will take
                     notes during meetings, workshops, conventions, conferences, etc. Learn
                     how to hear the main ideas and how to question information in light of
                     your priorities.

VII. CONTINUING THE CONVERSATION BEYOND THE CLASSROOM
Creating opportunities for learners to become actively involved in the process of thinking, doing, and reflecting is a key role for the instructor. In addition to supporting the private dialogue between the textbook author and the student, you need to encourage students to share their thoughts with one another and with you, thus extending the conversation into the classroom setting. We believe that you must consciously connect the course content to

- the individual student's life,
- the broader academic community,
- the world in which we live—our global society.

Here are some ideas that can carry the conversation beyond the chapter activities.

GOAL: To connect the information to the individual student's life.

1. The goal of a university education is not simply to memorize what is already known. The goal is to think about and question what is known in light of the personal and diverse experiences of your students. Ask your students to identify a passion or concern they have in life (cure for cancer, automobiles, cooking, sports, etc.). Then, have them attend next week's classes with the following assignment: Take notes and then reread your notes with the following question in mind: *What connection is there between my passion or concern and the information presented in my classes?* When students begin to realize that they can connect what they are hearing and learning with the things they care about, then taking notes can be an easier task.

2. Ask your students if they have ever read their doctor's notes about them. How important is accuracy? What would they expect to find? Why might they need to read what the doctor has said?

GOAL: To connect the information to the programs and practices in the broader academic community.

1. Identify a specific campus or community event and create a set of questions about the impact of this occurrence. Pair up your students, and have each pair interview different individuals in attendance about their reactions to this event. Then in class, have your students write a collaborative article about the event that could be submitted to a newspaper or posted as a blog. Tell them that the article will need quotes (this means that they will have to be accurate) and a balanced approach to the topic. Concise, accurate notes take on an urgency when there are such responsibilities.

2. Have your students create a workshop on note taking to share with high school students or other group of students on their campus. Suggest that they consider being a tutor and share this skill with others.

3. Another excellent assignment is to assign study groups. This is particularly relevant with learning communities. Each member of the study group can take

responsibility for analyzing and compiling notes for other members at a specific time during the semester.

GOAL: To connect to the global society.

1. History has been changed because someone did not get the right message. Ask your students to research and report on an historical event that resulted from misinformation, inappropriate translation, or other mistake in sharing knowledge. What role did a person's notes (or lack thereof) play in this event?

VIII.   CLASSROOM ACTIVITIES TO SUPPORT TEACHING THIS CHAPTER
- Admit/Exit Cards
- ¼ to ¾ or Recall Method of Note Taking
- Using Films in College Classrooms; see also AIE

ADMIT/EXIT CARDS

There are many variations on this idea. Consider which of these ideas appeal to you; mix and match ideas or create your own. Here are some examples:

1. To be admitted to class, students are told ahead of time that they must arrive with a question about the topic to be discussed that day. The teacher arrives early and collects the card with the question at the door. No card, no admittance.

2. In the syllabus, students are informed that they must write a 3 to 5 sentence paragraph responding to the prompt, "Since the last class, I have observed or accomplished the following about my educational goals…." The card with this paragraph is due at the beginning of each class period and must include the student's name and the date. Not only does this promote reflective thinking about learning but also it creates a private conversation between the faculty member and the student. Furthermore, the faculty member can use the cards to determine class attendance and when the cards are returned, the student has a record of his/her attendance as well.

3. Students are requested to record what they have read since the last class (be it required or for pleasure) and to provide comments about their readings. Placed on a 3×5 card, with the student's name and date, this card is taken up at the beginning of each class.

4. At the end of each class, students have to provide a card in order to leave. Request your students to do one of the following:
   - write a summary of the day's lesson.
   - write one question that has been left unanswered about the day's topic.
   - make an observation about how today's lecture applies to another class.
   - define a keyword that summarizes the lesson.
   - critique the instructor's teaching.

- o critique the student's participation.
- o identify the "muddiest point" from the lecture.
- o suggest what the next class topic should or will be.

$^1/_4$ to $^3/_4$ or RECALL SYSTEM OF NOTE TAKING

This is a lecture/activity to use in teaching the skill of note taking and particularly the 1/4-3/4 or Recall System. (This has also been called the Cornell system.)

Step 1. Ask students to take out a blank sheet of paper. Tell them to draw a line from the top to the bottom of the page, approximately $^1/_4$ of the way over from the left margin. Point out that this line is beyond the pink or red margin indicator on normal lined paper. Additionally, they should draw a horizontal line approximately one inch from the bottom of the page. They should then place their names, the date, and "page 1" in the upper right hand corner. Next, ask them to place the lecture topic across the top line of the page (the lecture topic for today is "note taking.") Inform them that during the lecture, they should "take notes the way they normally take notes, unless they do not normally take notes, in which case they should for today's purposes" in the area labeled "Notes, Notes, Notes." See illustration that follows:

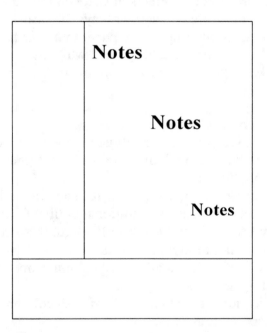

Step 2. Begin to lecture on the topic of note taking through the following series of questions and information. Encourage your students to answer these questions as you provide additional information. Be certain to observe whether students are writing down details and point out to them that it is important to take notes during this exercise.
Questions to ask:

Why should we take notes?
Possible answers: to remember, to enhance concentration, to help you study
What should good notes include?

Possible answers: main points, important terms, definitions, topic, class date, abbreviations (ask them to identify their favorite ones), graphics, diagrams, pictures, and blank space. At this point, define the purpose of blank space as a place to "go back to" and fill in with new information or thoughts; blank space also serves the purpose of making our notes look less confusing and more inviting.

A good example of how blank space works is to suggest that if given a choice between reading a copy Homer's *Odyssey* with tiny print and skinny little margins or the very same text in a much thicker book with large print and wide margins, which would they rather do? Most students will say they would prefer the larger text because it is easier to read even though it is a "bigger book." The same idea is true with our notes; blank space makes our notes easier to revise or think about when we return to them.

What skills do you need for taking good notes?
Possible answers: listening skills, concentration, and neatness/legibility for the note taker, organization skills, and active participation skills. Don't hesitate to point out that notes are highly personal and that words or phrases that one person hears and considers useful might be different than those words or phrases that another person might need for remembering the same information. This is one reason that using someone else's notes might not be helpful. At this point, it is useful to encourage your students to write on only one side of the paper–never on the back side. Suggest that there are many other ways they can work to save trees and the environment rather than through scrimping on the paper that they take notes. (I often guarantee that I will provide them with all of the paper they need while they are in college if they promise not to take notes on the back. So far, no one has taken me up on the offer, but I will happily do so if that is what it takes.)

Identify some of the known note taking structures.
Possible answers: as students give you answers, illustrate them on the board.
Outline: most students will be familiar with this one and will suggest that this is the one they use, if they use anything specific
Modified Outline: use of indentations, dashes, a few Roman numerals, major topics, and details but not nearly as formal as the traditional outline form
Mind Maps/Diagrams: a few students might be familiar with this structure because of writing papers in high school English courses
Split Page: one sheet of paper with two equally sized columns–one for lecture notes, the other for corresponding text notes
Matrix: just like the multiplication table chart—a chart with columns and rows of topics that meet with corresponding information
Paragraph/Summary: "the stenographer's style"; does not require thought but does require a fast hand
$\frac{1}{4}$ to $\frac{3}{4}$ or Recall Method or Cornell System: the one we are using today and the one most highly recommended because it allows you to save time, encourages you to interact with your notes, and promotes learning

What are some ways you can use your notes after class to help you recall information?
Possible answers: read them out loud, have others quiz you, rewrite them, re-list main ideas, rework them, place information in chronological order, make a test from them, develop questions from and about them.

Your students should now have sheets of paper that look similar to the following:

	Name Date Pg. 1 Note taking Take notes: to remember, stay awake, help me study, enhance concentration Good notes include: main pts., imp. terms, topic, definitions, date, my name, class name, abbreviations, graphics, diagrams, blank space Skills needed: listening, concentration, legibility, organization Common structures: outline, modified outline, mind maps/diagram, summary/paragraph, matrix, $^1/_4$ to $^3/_4$ or recall (Cornell system) Ways to review notes: out loud, quiz, rewrite, list main ideas, rework, place in chronological order, make test, create questions

Step 3: Tell your students that during the next three to five minutes, they will have an opportunity to rework these notes in a fashion that can save time when they need to study for a test. In the left hand column (the $^1/_4$ side) they should write questions that are answered by the information in the right-hand column (the $^3/_4$ side). In the bottom section, they should write

main terms summarizing important points in the lecture. At the end of this period, they should have sheets that look like the following:

	Name Date Pg. 1
	Note taking
Why take notes?	Take notes: to remember, stay awake, help me study, enhance concentration
What is included in good notes?	Good notes include: main pts., imp. terms, topic, definitions, date, my name, class name, abbreviations, graphics, diagrams, blank space
What skills are needed?	Skills needed: listening, concentration, legibility, organization
What are some NT structures?	Common structures: outline, modified outline, diagram/mind maps, summary/paragraph, matrix, $^1/_4$ to $^3/_4$ or recall (Cornell system)
How can I review my notes?	Ways to Review notes: out loud, quiz, rewrite, list main ideas, rework, place in chronological order, make test, create questions
Important Terms: Blank space, main terms, mind maps, matrix, ¼—¾ or Recall (Cornell), review	

Step 4. Now comes the fun part of this lecture. Ask the students to cover up their notes. What do they have in front of them? (They should be able to respond that they have a quiz.) Ask them how long it took to review their notes in this way. Usually, it takes 2 to 4 minutes for approximately 15 to 20 minutes of lecture (the approximate length of this particular lecture).

What value would using this technique have? How could it save them time when studying? How could they use it to review information? Usually, your students will be able to state all of the positive reasons for using this structure. These benefits include not only a place for all of the elements found in useful notes (date, topic, blank space, diagrams, etc.) but also an awareness that the structure does not depend on the faculty member being organized. The reason that the outline form usually fails in a college classroom is because faculty become sidetracked by questions and end up discussing information out of order–this system easily accommodates that occurrence.

This is a great place to be dramatic about note taking. Ask your students if they know where knowledge comes from. (Often they will say that it comes from books, other people, your lectures, from within, etc.) Tell them that these are good guesses but do they really know where knowledge comes from. Allow them to struggle with this question. Then, push forward and ask them: What are some of the problems that we are facing that we have not solved? Ask each person to identify a concern–usually they will say things like AIDS, cancer, child abuse, the environment, war, etc. Tell them that we know lots of information about each of these issues but why haven't we solved these problems yet. Try to get them to say "because we don't have all of the answers yet or we don't have enough knowledge" or something similar.

Then, repeat the question from before: "So, where will this new knowledge come from?" With any luck, you should have them stumped and wondering about the answer. This is exactly the mood you want–students thinking about the topic. You might ask them if they want to know where it comes from and even have them raise their hands if they do. After you have their attention and with as much belief as you can muster tell them that knowledge is born of questions. Your students will probably be let down a little to know that this is what you have been driving at so you need to be convincing that this is a terrific discovery because everyone can ask questions.

Indeed, the hard part is learning to ask the right questions and that is why a note taking method that allows them to practice asking questions is such an important strategy to use. It is possible that if they spend time with the right question, they can come up with more and/or different answers than the ones the teacher has and that is exactly how new knowledge is created or becomes known. Stress that this is the first step to critical thinking and a note taking method that allows them to practice critical thinking is extremely useful.

Then, ask them why they won't use this technique. Despite how wonderful this structure is in providing for everything that they have just discussed as being important to taking good notes, they will not readily embrace a system they have not already used. Part of the reason they are hesitant to change their present system is because "what they do got them into college." Also, habits are simply difficult to change without real reason; grades on their first tests often send students in search of new ways. Another reason they won't use this system is because it takes more paper. They cannot get everything they need to write in the space provided by the $^3/_4$ column. (For this one, suggest that they use the back of the previous page for writing questions; remember, they can't take notes on the back side, so this is a great place to put the review questions and important terms.) Allow them to state what they will have difficulty with but in the end, require them to take notes using this system in at least your class and one other class for the next three weeks. At the end of that time, you should look at, grade, and evaluate their notes. Your goal is to teach them a system and then they can decide if it helps them or is of use to them.

USING FILMS IN COLLEGE CLASSROOMS

Films are extremely appropriate to use in college classrooms and can often illustrate a point better than your words and actions. Consider using films for any of the following reasons:

1. To promote discussion about a value or theme relevant to college life and your course,
2. To provide a source of information for your students to practice listening skills, concentration skills, note taking skills, test taking skills or other study skills,
3. To accommodate students with different learning styles,
4. To appeal to students who have grown up in a multi-media culture.

Films provide students with yet another way to sharpen their understanding of how they recall information. They may begin to associate that facts are easier to recall if presented with multiple images of an idea—visually, auditory, verbally, etc.

Be cautious about using films that are dated through dress or language unless you are willing for those elements to override the message you want your students to hear. Ask your colleagues and former students to assist you in creating a list of films that meet your needs. Take the time to view these films before showing them so that you can be prepared to address sensitive issues.

Chapter 4

Taking Tests

I. CHAPTER SUMMARY

Learning outcomes for this chapter

LO 4.1   Identify what kinds of tests you will take in college
LO 4.2   Explain the best ways to prepare for and take various kinds of tests
LO 4.3   Discuss the strategies for answering specific kinds of test questions

Message to the student

Life is a series of tests. The preparation and performance process that you use in school will serve you the rest of your life. Spend the time now to develop and practice a process that encourages you to learn with confidence and joy. Grades on tests reflect the mastery (or lack thereof) of a finite amount of information. Different types of tests can be tackled best through a variety of strategies but techniques for performing well on tests mean nothing without personal integrity. This characteristic reflects your willingness not just to be honest about everything you say and do but also to hold yourself accountable in all matters.

Challenging yourself to set an example and expecting the very best of those around you is both a personal and public value. Your preparation process reflects both your character and your integrity. Your knowledge base is evaluated by your performance on tests—in college classrooms, the evaluation is a summary of how quickly and logically you can assimilate a variety of facts and thoughts about an abstract situation. After college, the evaluation is based on your demonstration of how information can be applied to very real situations. The ethics you apply in college will reflect those you use beyond the classroom.

Message to the instructor

Parker Palmer shares that teaching is more than a collection of techniques and tips. It is the embodiment and reflection of the personal integrity of the teacher. This chapter provides an excellent opportunity to discuss the issue of academic integrity and personal character, although it is by no means the only place to have these discussions. Research suggests that cheating is not only widespread but also is openly accepted to get ahead. Our world has been inundated with decades of public disclosure of moral failings whether they are corporate, governmental, or personal. Such lapses raise the question: why be honest?

College students report a high incidence of academic dishonesty from their high school years and many indicate they plan to continue that practice in college. This cavalier attitude erodes public confidence in the purpose and meaning of a college degree and bodes poorly for a nation's interactions in a global environment. You can assist your students in their daily work to be honest citizens. Hold them accountable for high quality work and expect them to be able to show you how they created and completed assignments. One of our most important tasks is to model academic integrity with our students and follow up on this issue throughout the course. You may want to discuss your institution's code of student conduct or honor code at this time.

II.   KEY IDEAS AND CONCEPTS TO CONSIDER
Refer also to key terms listed in back of chapter.

academic honesty
academic integrity code
code of student conduct
direction words
ethics
honor code
objective
personal integrity
subjective
test anxiety

III.   CLARIFYING QUESTIONS AND DISCUSSION PROMPTS
At the end of each chapter in the Annotated Instructor's Edition (AIE), teaching tips, discussion prompts, student alerts and additional exercises and activities are organized around specific learning outcomes. These questions can be used to encourage class discussion, small group work, and/or individual reflection about the information presented in this chapter.

1.   How can you improve your test preparation?
2.   Discuss the activities, strategies, thought processes, beliefs, and/or self-talk that you engage in when preparing for a test.
3.   How much time do you spend preparing for tests?
4.   What do you believe is meant by the term "academic integrity"?
5.   How do you really feel about your peers cheating? About yourself cheating?
6.   What are the consequences for academic dishonesty at your institution?
7.   Why are tests given?
8.   What does it mean to fail a test? What does it mean to do well on a test?
9.   How do tests truly reflect real-life situations?

IV.   CLASSROOM ACTIVITIES AND ASSIGNMENTS
Consider using the following exercises when teaching this chapter. Always refer to the Instructor's Annotations at the end of each chapter in the AIE. Those listed below with an asterisk (*) can be found at the end of this chapter in Section VIII; those with a double asterisk (**) are in the student text. Others are self-explanatory.

Copyright © 2011 by The McGraw-Hill Companies, Inc.

The first three activities are particularly well suited for learning communities. If you have formed study groups in your learning communities, assign these tasks to those groups.

*Create a **pre-test** with your students for an upcoming test in this course or have them prepare one for another course. (1 to 2 hours, in and out of class)
Generate possible test questions from class notes—refer back to note taking styles that make this process easier.
*Use the **post-exam survey** to spark discussion and examination after an exam—either yours or one from another class
*Admit/Exit Cards (5 to 10 minutes, out of class)
*Jigsaw (30 to 45 minutes, in class)
*Using Films in College Classrooms (30 to 45 minutes, in class); see also AIE
**Journal Reflections (15 minutes, in class) Have your students refer back to the Myers-Briggs Type Inventory or other learning styles inventory and use the information about preferred learning styles to discuss how they prefer to prepare for tests.
**TRY IT! 4 (20 minutes, in or out of class)

V.   USING THE P.O.W.E.R. LEARNING PROCESS IN YOUR INSTRUCTION
Whether you are learning to learn or learning to teach, Bob Feldman's P.O.W.E.R. Learning process is a useful tool. Here are our ideas for applying this process as an instructor with this chapter.

P.repare: Write your syllabus with this chapter in mind. Plan to cover the material in this chapter one to two weeks prior to the first major test/exam in class. Point out this connection to students in the first days of class. Or, if you are part of a learning community, make this a shared assignment with your linked class.

O.rganize: Plan to use the Jigsaw activity (described in Section VIII) during the class when you teach this information. This means you need to prepare the role expectation guidelines, coded cards, and signs for the classroom so that students will move from the learning group to the teaching group. Ask students to read this chapter prior to coming to class.

W.ork: JIGSAW: This is a learning activity that provides an opportunity for all students to learn information and be responsible for sharing their knowledge with others. This work can also be done within study groups.

E.valuate: The test on this chapter or in your linked class is the ultimate evaluation of how students learned.

R.ethink: Provide the post-exam survey and take time to go over their survey results prior to giving back their tests. Ask them how they would prepare differently for the next test, based on their survey responses, and their test grades. Remember the key element in change: if students are receiving the grades they want, they will not change their study behaviors or habits.

TRY IT! In the space below, begin a teaching journal of the ideas that worked and changes you would make the next time you teach this topic.

_____

_____

_____

_____

_____

_____

_____

_____

VI.   CONNECTIONS WITHIN THE TEXT
        Consider bringing up this chapter's ideas again in the following contexts:

        Chapter 1   how you learn is reflected in how you prefer to think. How you
                      recall is a learning process. No one recalls information without
                      practice.
        Chapter 3   the note taking strategy used by students can enhance or hinder their
                      ability to study for a test; this is an excellent skill to re-evaluate at this
                      time.
        Chapter 5   memory skills result from review of information
        Chapter 6   connect test preparation to preparing for work-related tasks and
                      expectations
        Chapter 10   connect test preparation to stress reduction

VII.   CONTINUING THE CONVERSATION BEYOND THE CLASSROOM
        Creating opportunities for learners to become actively involved in the process of
        thinking, doing, and reflecting is a key role for the instructor. In addition to supporting
        the private dialogue between the textbook author and the student, you need to encourage

students to share their thoughts with one another and with you; thus, extending the conversation into the classroom setting. We believe that you must consciously connect the course content to

- the individual student's life,
- the programs and practices of the broader academic community,
- the world in which we live—our global society.

Here are some ideas that can carry the conversation beyond the chapter activities.

GOAL: To connect the information to the individual student's life.

1.   Ask your students to identify the different ways they have been tested/evaluated/assessed in life. Tell them to think beyond their academic life. What values, actions, behaviors, beliefs are tested by life?

2.   In small groups, discuss the concepts of failure and success. How do they recognize failure and success that is not associated with a grade? How will they know if they are successful or failures in the workforce?

3.   Most clubs and organizations require its members to learn and be tested on specific information (history, founding members, oaths, codes, etc.). Have your students ever needed to learn such information for personal reasons? How did they prepare? What feelings and concerns did they have? How was this similar to or different from their experiences with academic tests? Could they transfer this information from a service/social context to an academic one?

GOAL: To connect the information to the programs and practices in the broader academic community.

1.   Define integrity. Ask students to define the unique role of integrity within the academic community. Is it really necessary? Why or why not?

2.   Ask students to identify as many types of cheating as they know (plagiarism, dual submission of papers, etc.) Ask students to review the academic integrity code of your institution and compare it to the code of another. Are there any similarities or differences among the definitions used by another school?

3.   What is a portfolio? How is it different, better, or worse than more traditional assessment tools such as tests and term papers?

4.   What consequences exist for cheating on college assignments? Do you believe they are justified?

GOAL: To connect to the global society.

1.   The American educational system relies on several types of tests to suggest that students have learned information. Ask students to compare the educational tests and assessments used in European and/or Asian settings.

2.   What are the real tests of knowledge? What events, moments, and policies have tested the abilities of world leaders? How did your students determine success or failure in these terms? Was there agreement among all of your students? What implications does agreement/disagreement have in such circumstances?

3. What differences exist between an individual choosing to cheat on his/her taxes and a multi-billion international corporation doing so?

4. Is there such a thing as environmental ethics? How have past generations' decisions about the planet determined your fate?

VIII. CLASSROOM ACTIVITIES TO SUPPORT TEACHING THIS CHAPTER
- Pre-test
- Post-exam Survey
- Admit/Exit Cards
- Jigsaw
- Using Films in College Classrooms; see also AIE

PRE-TEST

One of the more productive test preparation activities is the creation of a pre-test. Not only does it serve as an organizational strategy for course materials and assignments but also it provides students with a means for organizing their thinking about course ideas. The process is quite simple and students report that it really works.

Step 1. Students should create a cover sheet for the pre-test with the following information on it:

Pre-test Cover Sheet

Name of Course:
Date of Exam:
Name of Professor:
List of Books, Articles, Films, and/or Handouts Pertinent to This Test
List of Key Concepts, Individuals, Places, Events and/or Dates

Step 2: Students should create a five-part test for any test coming up in the next few weeks, using the materials listed on the cover sheet. In order to encourage them to think about information in more than one way, it helps to assign several different types of questions for them to use in developing this assignment. An example of this would be:

Section I	5 short answer questions (2 points each)
Section II	10 multiple-choice questions (2 points each)
Section III	20 matching questions (1 point each)
Section IV	10 true/false questions (1 point each)
Section V	4 essay questions—choose 2 to answer (20 points each)

The practice of creating a test *is* studying in and of itself. You can choose to evaluate their pre-tests or simply have them evaluate each other's pre-tests. The act of taking their own or someone else's pre-test is simply one more way to refresh their memory of the information.

POST-EXAM SURVEY

After a test has been completed, it is useful to encourage your students to evaluate the strategies they used in preparing for the test. It is particularly useful to complete this survey prior to receiving their test results because it allows them to assess better their intuition about their test performance. If they are not satisfied with their test results then they have an accounting of the specific set of activities they used and can decide what they might need to do differently in the future. This simple set of questions begins this process.

1. The easiest part of the test for me was …
2. The most difficult part of the test for me was …
3. The mindset (confident, surprised, anxious, etc.) that I had when I took the test was …
4. The mindset that I had when I completed the test was ….
5. The study methods I used in preparing for this test included: (check all that apply)
    _____ attended all classes
    _____ attended all labs
    _____ took notes at all lectures and labs
    _____ completed all assignments (reading, problem solving, etc.)
    _____ completed most of the assignments (reading, problem solving, etc.)
    _____ completed a few of the assignments (reading, problem solving, etc.)
    _____ created a pre-test
    _____ studied with classmates
    _____ studied alone
    _____ met with my instructor
    _____ attended scheduled study sessions
    _____ met with a tutor or Supplemental Instruction leader
    _____ other (please list):
6. The number of hours I spent preparing for this test was _____.
7. What grade do you believe you earned on this test?
8. (After you have received your test back): What grade did you receive?
9. How would you prepare for the next test? What changes would you make?

ADMIT/EXIT CARDS

There are many variations on this idea. Consider which of these ideas appeal to you; mix and match ideas or create your own. Here are some examples:

1. To be admitted to class, students are told ahead of time that they must arrive with a question about the topic to be discussed that day. The teacher arrives early and collects the card with the question at the door. No card, no admittance.
2. In the syllabus, students are informed that they must write a 3 to 5 sentence paragraph responding to the prompt, "Since the last class, I have observed or accomplished the following about my educational goals…." The card with this paragraph is due at the beginning of each class period and must include the student's name and the date. Not only does this promote reflective thinking about learning but also it creates a private

conversation between the faculty member and the student. Furthermore, the faculty member can use the cards to determine class attendance and when the cards are returned, the student has a record of his/her attendance as well.

3. Students are requested to record what they have read since the last class (be it required or for pleasure) and to provide comments about their readings. Placed on a 3×5 card, with the student's name and date, this card is taken up at the beginning of each class.

4. At the end of each class, students have to provide a card in order to leave. Request your students to do one of the following:
    - write a summary of the day's lesson.
    - write one question that has been left unanswered about the day's topic.
    - make an observation about how today's lecture applies to another class.
    - define a keyword that summarizes the lesson.
    - critique the instructor's teaching.
    - critique the student's participation.
    - identify the "muddiest point" from the lecture.
    - suggest what the next class topic should or will be.

JIGSAW

Sometimes it helps to model the active review of information in the classroom. Jigsawing is an exercise used by educators to illustrate the results of collaborative learning. The premise is simple: have multiple groups, with each group developing expert knowledge for one aspect of an assignment. Then, have a representative member from each of the first groups meet together in a second group to share the expert knowledge of all aspects. This provides a complete review of the information and gives every student a chance to participate. Another reason for using this particular strategy is that is supports the notion of shared responsibility for learning.

Step 1. Assign a common reading, viewing of a film, or attendance at a discussion or presentation.

Step 2. During class, place students in a group and assign a specific, different set of questions/concepts for each group to answer and master. Allow your students to spend up to 10 minutes developing answers or definitions about their topic. Make it clear that each member of the group must know as much as every other member of the group since they will be "lone representatives" in the next phase of this activity.

Step 3. After a specific amount of time, reconfigure your groups so that one representative from each of the first groups is a member of the second group. Give them a specified amount of time to share what they know. Let them know that they will be evaluated at the end of this group work.

Step 4. You should now evaluate your students. Tests, written assignment, or open class discussion are ways to determine how much information your students understood.

USING FILMS IN COLLEGE CLASSROOMS

Films are extremely appropriate to use in college classrooms and can often illustrate a point better than your words and actions. Consider using films for any of the following reasons:

5. To promote discussion about a value or theme relevant to college life and your course
6. To provide a source of information for your students to practice listening skills, concentration skills, note taking skills, test taking skills, or other study skills
7. To accommodate students with different learning styles
8. To appeal to students who have grown up in a multi-media culture.

Films provide students with yet another way to sharpen their understanding of how they recall information. They may begin to associate that facts are easier to recall if presented with multiple images of an idea—visually, auditory, verbally, etc.

Be cautious about using films that are dated through dress or language unless you are willing for those elements to override the message you want your students to hear. Ask your colleagues and former students to assist you in creating a list of films that meet your needs. Take the time to view these films before showing them so that you can be prepared to address sensitive issues.

Chapter 5

Reading and Remembering

I.   CHAPTER SUMMARY

Learning objectives for this chapter

LO 5.1   Identify the essential elements of successful reading
LO 5.2   Explain how to improve concentration and read more effectively
LO 5.3   Discuss techniques for memorizing large amounts of information
LO 5.4   Analyze how best to retain what you have read

Message to the student

      When you consider all of the ways we try to process the world, reading is often overlooked or ignored in favor of speaking, watching, or listening. Yet it can be among the valuable ways to practice your analytical, reflection, and memory skills. Reading allows you to practice disciplined, logical thinking without the haste or clatter of other voices that exist in heated classroom discussions. However, the reading skills that worked for you in elementary and high school may not be adequate for college-level work. In college you will be expected to read more information without regular opportunities to review or clarify the reading, unless you ask. It is easy, in the beginning, to believe that the readings don't matter because your professor did not discuss them in class. Nothing could be further from the truth. You are supposed to connect the readings to the information presented in class. You need to read.

      Equally important is the ability to recall information—particularly information that you read. This chapter provides you with ways to enhance your memory skills through the development of organizational structures. Each person has an amazing capacity for memory and we can recall extraordinary amounts of information and detail. Much of the routine knowledge we hold, we take for granted. Imagine what it would be like to have to relearn our daily patterns every day! We often consider ourselves stupid and begin down the path of self-doubt and failure when we cannot remember exactly what we want at the moment we need it. The truth is that our level of engagement with a subject is often the key to our ability to recall it. That is why it is important to take heart in the idea that your memory can be improved.

Message to the instructor

      The written word—and the ability of our students to comprehend it—is a cornerstone to academic success. One key to enhancing this skill of your students is to find a way to make them believe that they still have a great deal to learn about being better readers. Remember, most college students haven't had instruction in reading since the fifth grade. It is critical that you stress that college instructors expect students to be readers and seldom is there time to review the reading material in class. This is a major shift in class preparation for your students.

Attention span is another critical focus point in this chapter. Much has been said and written about the shortening of attention span in children who have been raised on sound bytes and computer games. Certainly the increase in attention-deficit disorder (ADD) and attention-deficit hyperactivity disorder (ADHD) and use of medication reflects this concern. This chapter provides the opportunity to slow down and examine some of our fundamental behaviors in a new light.

Finally, ways to assist students improve their ability to recall information are found throughout this chapter. The goal is not to help students discover new ways to memorize lots of facts and details but to become aware of the factors that influence or improve their recall of experiences and information. The notion of over-learning is discussed—the distinction between surface learning and deep learning. Insist that your students grapple with the notion that the more time
and energy spent applying information will directly impact their ability to remember it.

II.   KEY IDEAS AND CONCEPTS TO CONSIDER
      Refer also to key terms listed in back of chapter.

      attention span
      margin notes
      memory consolidation
      mnemonics
      reading style
      recall
      retrieval
      review
      scanning
      skimming
      Summer Reading/Common Book Program
      visualization

III. CLARIFYING QUESTIONS AND DISCUSSION PROMPTS
      At the end of each chapter in the Annotated Instructor's Edition (AIE), teaching tips, discussion prompts, student alerts and additional exercises and activities are organized around specific learning outcomes. These questions can be used to encourage class discussion, small group work, and/or individual reflection about the information presented in this chapter.

      1.   What was the best book you read last year that was not an academic assignment?
      2.   When did you discover this semester that you were behind in your reading? Have there been any negative consequences for not reading assignments?
      3.   Have you ever suffered from or known someone who suffered from a disability that made reading difficult, if not impossible?
      4.   Why might you have problems with memory, and how do you deal with these problems?

5. Can you think of a time when you remembered everything you wanted to recall? What made this possible?

6. What role does concentration play in your ability to recall or forget information?

IV. CLASSROOM ACTIVITIES AND ASSIGNMENTS
Consider using the following exercises when teaching this chapter. Always refer to the Instructor's Annotations at the end of each chapter in the AIE. Those listed below with an asterisk (*) can be found at the end of this chapter in Section VIII; those with a double asterisk (**) are in the student text. Others are self-explanatory.

*Admit/Exit Cards (5 to 10 minutes, out of class)
*Teaching a novel as part of the course (several class sessions)
*Faculty Reading Interview (30 minutes, out of class); see also AIE
*Using Films in the College Classroom
*Common Book or Summer Reading Program
*Memory Tray (15 minutes, in class)
*Words and Shapes Activity (20 minutes, in class)
**Try It! 2 (15-20 minutes, in class)
**Try It! 5 (15 minutes, in class)
**Try It! 6 (15 minutes, in class)

V. USING THE P.O.W.E.R. LEARNING PROCESS IN YOUR INSTRUCTION
Whether you are learning to learn or learning to teach, Bob Feldman's P.O.W.E.R. Learning process is a useful tool. Here are our ideas for applying this process as an instructor with this chapter.

P.repare: A common reading assignment is very useful in teaching this chapter. There are several possibilities: 1) a short article on some topic that is current and pertinent to your campus, i.e., campus politics, health and wellness issues, or even background information on a visiting lecturer; 2) a textbook from another class in which many or all of your students are also enrolled, or 3) a novel or other supplemental book that is part of your course requirements. Consider using any collaborative teaching/learning technique you already know or have read about in the other chapters (such as Jigsaw).

O.rganize: Have your class divide themselves into groups based on the collaborative technique you select (for a reading activity, three to five students per group is good). For this class, plan to use an entire class for a collaborative reading activity; this is a practical concern as well as an indication of the value you place on reading.

W.ork: Now the work begins. Each group must decide how to tackle their reading assignment and demonstrate the reading technique they used. Allow at least half the class period for this part of the work. With 15 to 20 minutes left in the class, ask one member from each group to demonstrate the technique they used.

While the students are working, you should be moving from group to group to observe and offer suggestions. Remember, we talk a lot about collaborative learning but that does not mean that students know how to do it.

E.valuate: First, the students need to evaluate whether the reading techniques they applied worked for them and other members of their group. Did they have enough time to complete the assignment in class? Ask students how they could apply what they learned about reading to another class or another text. How does their technique enhance their ability to remember? Make them write one intention statement they agree to apply to a reading assignment in another class. Allow time the following week for students to report on their progress in this area.

R.ethink: Students are often resistant to learning and applying new study skills. The reason it is hard is that most faculty prefer a developmental approach rather than a coercive assignment. First year students are like kids, "You have to make them take that first bite of broccoli even if they don't eat the whole serving." Do you think you made that happen in this class period? Were you comfortable with the chaos that this kind of applied exercise creates in your class? Were your students successful in working collaboratively? What do you need to do to develop this skill so that your class is able to reap the benefits of a working class period?

TRY IT! In the space below, begin a teaching journal of the ideas that worked and changes you would make the next time you teach this topic.

_____

_____

_____

_____

_____

_____

VI. CONNECTIONS WITHIN THE TEXT
Consider bringing up this chapter's ideas again in the following contexts:

Chapter 1	memory is connected to learning style preferences
Chapter 2	time management is easier when using the same block of time for the same activity each day
Chapter 3	link reading and taking notes
Chapter 4	link reading and preparing for tests
Chapter 6	link reading to discovering information about career choices and staying informed at work
Chapter 10	link reading as a pleasurable habit that can alleviate stress

VII. CONTINUING THE CONVERSATION BEYOND THE CLASSROOM
Creating opportunities for learners to become actively involved in the process of thinking, doing, and reflecting is a key role for the instructor. In addition to supporting the private dialogue between the textbook author and the student, you need to encourage students to share their thoughts with one another and with you; thus, extending the conversation into the classroom setting. We believe that you must consciously connect the course content to

- the individual student's life,
- the programs and practices in the broader academic community,
- the world in which we live—our global society.

Here are some ideas that can carry the conversation beyond the chapter activities.

GOAL: To connect the information to the individual student's life.

1. Have your students pair up and visit each other's regular study space. Tell them to write an essay reflecting how the space supports or hinders the occupant's ability to read and remember. They can turn the essay in or you can use it as a prompt for a class discussion.

2. Ask each student to identify something they can do without thinking. Then ask them to think about how long and why they began the process of learning that information. How long have they spent learning it? How many ways have they practiced it, observed it, thought about it, made mistakes with it, read about it or talked about it. What does this suggest about learning and memory? Allow them to share this with another person in class.

GOAL: To connect the information to the programs and practices in the broader academic community.

1.   Assign the Faculty Reading Interview for an enlightening discussion about reading habits of a favorite faculty member.
2.   If your campus has a Summer Reading or Common Book program, encourage your students to participate in the activities that serve to bring the text alive. If you don't have such a program, have your students explore programs on other campuses in order to initiate one on their own campus.
3.   Discuss the elements of technology (e.g., Web bulletins, electronic boards, text messaging, etc.) used on your campus to remind students of all that is occurring. Of these, which do your students consider the most effective and why?

GOAL: To connect to the global society.

1.   Take an international incident and have students read about it in a statewide, national, and international newspaper. Are the stories different? How so? How do these differences shape their thinking about the event?
2.   Compare your understanding of an event as portrayed on television and covered in a newspaper. Are there substantial differences? Which do you believe is more reliable? Why?
3.   Culture is the collective memory of a group of people. What ways do societies have for remembering their past and absorbing the lessons of their culture? Ask students to explore this through the lessons of one culture.

VIII.   CLASSROOM ACTIVITIES TO SUPPORT TEACHING THIS CHAPTER
   • Admit/Exit Cards
   • Teaching a Novel or other Supplemental Reading
   • Faculty Reading Interview; see also AIE
   • Using Films in the College Classroom
   • Common Book or Summer Reading Program
   • Memory Tray
   • Words and Shapes Activity

Teaching reading skills can be done through a variety of approaches that also allow you to address issues such as interpersonal development, the transition from high school to college, goal setting, and relationships. The activities suggested for this chapter are starting points for assisting students in organizing their thoughts and feelings about these ideas.

ADMIT/EXIT CARDS

There are many variations on this idea. Consider which of these ideas appeal to you; mix and match ideas or create your own. Here are some examples:

1. To be admitted to class, students are told ahead of time that they must arrive with a question about the topic to be discussed that day. The teacher arrives early and collects the card with the question at the door. No card, no admittance.

2. In the syllabus, students are informed that they must write a three to five sentence paragraph responding to the prompt, "Since the last class, I have observed or accomplished the following about my educational goals…." The card with this paragraph is due at the beginning of each class period and must include the student's name and the date. Not only does this promote reflective thinking about learning but also it creates a private conversation between the faculty member and the student. Furthermore, the faculty member can use the cards to determine class attendance and when the cards are returned, the student has a record of his/her attendance as well.

3. Students are requested to record what they have read since the last class (be it required or for pleasure) and to provide comments about their readings. Placed on a 3 × 5 index card, with the student's name and date, this card is taken up at the beginning of each class.

4. At the end of each class, students have to provide a card in order to leave. Request your students to do one of the following:
    - write a summary of the day's lesson.
    - write one question that has been left unanswered about the day's topic.
    - make an observation about how today's lecture applies to another class.
    - define a keyword that summarizes the lesson.
    - critique the instructor's teaching.
    - critique the student's participation.
    - identify the "muddiest point" from the lecture.
    - suggest what the next class topic should or will be.

TEACHING A NOVEL (or other Supplemental Reading)

The use of required reading, in addition to the main text, is a common teaching tool in student success courses. Obviously, there is pedagogical merit in assigning a reading but some of the less obvious reasons for the use of a novel or other supplemental reading are:
- common experience for the class; often certain words or characters become a part of the class vocabulary (shared experiences bond people together)
- discussion of personal issues without putting a student on the spot
- view of life through the eyes of another; this can lead to a discussion of the value of the humanities in education
- basis for comparison between one's own life and the one posed by the novel—basis for comparison between the concepts in the text and ideas in another book—such work promotes critical-thinking skill development

To be effective, readings should be discussed thoroughly and incorporated into class discourse. Supplemental readings can be the subject of writing assignments, class examinations, presentations, or projects. Encouraging students to read for pleasure, information, self-fulfillment, and/or personal development can be one of the most powerful contributions made by a student success course.

The following list of books is just a beginning. These particular books have been used in student success courses around the country but they are not the only ones to consider using.

Novel and Supplemental Reading Suggestions

A Home on the Field, Paul Cuadros
A Hope in the Unseen, Ron Suskind
A Lesson Before Dying, Ernest Gaines
All Quiet on the Western Front, Erich Maria Remarque
Cold Mountain, Charles Frazier
Ellen Foster, Kaye Gibbons
Ender's Game, Orson Scott Card
Freakonomics, Stephen Dubner and Steven Levitt
Growing Up, Russell Baker
I Know Why the Caged Bird Sings, Maya Angelou
In the Time of the Butterflies, Julia Alvarez
Night, Elie Wiesel
One Day in the Life of Ivan Denisovich, Alexander Solzhenitzyn
One L, Scott Turow
Oral History, Lee Smith
Raney, Clyde Edgerton
Siddhartha, Herman Hesse
The Art of Loving, Erich Fromm
The Education of Little Tree, Forrest Carter
The Grand Inquisitor, Fyodor Dostoyevsky
The Kite Runner, Khaled Hosseini
The Measure of Our Success, Marion Wright-Edelman
The Road Less Traveled, Scott Peck
The Things They Carried, Tim O'Brien
Tuesdays with Morrie, Mitch Albom
Way of the Peaceful Warrior, Dan Millman
Whisper of the River, Ferrol Sams
Zen and the Art of Motorcycle Maintenance, Robert M. Pirsig

Discussion Questions:
Many publishers provide reading guides as a result of community book discussion groups and college-based Common Book or Summer Reading programs. Such guides are readily available on the publisher's Web site for a particular book.

FACULTY READING INTERVIEW

Students do not readily communicate with faculty members outside of the classroom and some faculty would argue that they don't even communicate in the classroom. Encouraging students to develop relationships with faculty members is one of the single most important goals you can pursue in a student success course. This interview is a stepping-stone to developing the listening skills needed for two-way communication.

Require your students to consider thoughtfully which faculty member they would like to know more about—discourage them from interviewing you since you will have ample opportunity for talking and listening with your students in the class and through other activities. Remind them to follow basic courtesies such as requesting an appointment for the interview and being on time. The student should make certain that the faculty member knows beforehand what the appointment is about and he or she might even want to provide a copy of the questionnaire for the faculty member to read prior to the interview. Your students might suggest to the faculty member that they meet away from the departmental office for a cup of coffee or a light lunch in the cafeteria. However, they should be just as sensitive to and appreciative of a faculty member who might be more comfortable being interviewed in his or her office—many campuses have specific policies regarding the development of relationship between students and faculty. It may be important to tell your students to not attempt this interview over the telephone. Finally, encourage your students to end the interview with a thank you; a letter or note would not be necessary but a heartfelt "thank you for your time" would certainly be appropriate and greatly appreciated.

FACULTY READING INTERVIEW QUESTIONNAIRE

Student Name _____ Professor's Name _____
Date _____ Professor's Discipline _____

1. Where did you go to school, and how did you choose your particular field?

2. What was the first important book you read? Which other books have influenced your thinking? Why?

3. Do you remember the most challenging reading assignment you tackled? How did you handle it?

4. With all of the literature available to teach this and other courses, how do you decide which books to assign?

5. What newspapers do you read regularly?

6. Are there specific Web sites that you find more reliable than others for information?

7. What do you like to read for pleasure?

8. Where do you go when you want to find good books?

USING FILMS IN COLLEGE CLASSROOMS

Films are extremely appropriate to use in college classrooms and can often illustrate a point better than your words and actions. Consider using films for any of the following reasons:

- Promote discussion about a value or theme relevant to college life and your course.
- Provide a source of information for your students to practice listening, concentration, note taking, test taking, or other study skills.
- Accommodate students with different learning styles.
- Appeal to students who have grown up in a multimedia culture, etc.

Films provide students with yet another way to sharpen their understanding of how they recall information. They may begin to associate that facts are easier to recall if presented with multiple images of an idea—visually, auditory, verbally, etc.

Reading skills can be sharpened through the use of films. Consider asking students to compare the film version to the assigned text; acknowledge that you understand that students will often try to watch a film instead of reading the book. Students may need to be warned that significant differences often exist in the telling of a story on film.

Be cautious about using films that are "dated" through dress or language unless you are willing for those elements to override the message you want your students to hear. Ask your colleagues and former students to assist you in creating a list of films that meet your needs. Take the time to view these films before showing them so that you can be prepared to address sensitive issues.

COMMON BOOK OR SUMMER READING PROGRAM

Many efforts have been made in recent years to encourage people to read. One of the more important innovations on college campuses has been to assign a common reading (often over the summer) that is discussed throughout the academic year. This common reading assignment is usually established for an entire first year class although the entire campus (and sometimes the broader community) is invited to read the selection and to participate in discussions, speakers, presentations, and/or other activities that flesh out important themes or ideas. The reading selection can, for example, be integrated into classes, serve as the focus for a speaker series, guide theatre department productions, provide the basis for an academic conversation during orientation, and enhance the overall academic climate on your campus.

MEMORY TRAY

Many college students believe that a good memory is something determined at birth, much like whether they have brown or green eyes. The ability to recall information is a practiced habit that can be improved upon, with this exercise illustrating to students how memory can be sharpened.

Step 1. Outside of the classroom, assemble two trays with approximately 20 items on each tray. While it is fine to have some items (up to five) in common on both trays, it is best to have as many different items as possible. Find a variety of familiar and unfamiliar items to put on trays.

Step 2. During class, announce that you have several items that you would like for your students to view and attempt to recall. Bring in the tray and give them two minutes to look at the items, and then remove the tray and items.

Step 3. After the tray has been removed, ask them to draw the tray and to include as many items as they can recall; they can choose to write the name of some items if they wish, since drawing might take too much time. Give them two minutes for this task.

Step 4. Bring in the tray and assess the success of your class in identifying the items. Were they able to recall all of the items? Which ones were they most likely to recall? Can they suggest reasons why? On the board, list the strategies that different students used to recall the items.

Step 5. Bring in the second tray and this time, allow students to pick the items up, ask questions about them, move them around on the tray. You should allot at least 10 minutes for this activity. Then, remove the tray.

Step 6. After the tray has been removed, ask them to draw the second tray and to include as many items as they can recall; they can choose to write the name of some items if they wish since drawing might take too much time. Give them five minutes for this task.

Step 7. Bring in the second tray and assess the success of your class in identifying the items. Hopefully, they did better in identifying the items because they had more time with the items, familiarity with the task, the ability to reorganize, and ask questions about the items. Can your students suggest these factors? And more importantly, can they make a connection between these factors and a way to improve their retention of the information they are studying?

Step 8. (Optional) Ask your students to write a journal entry, reflection card, or reaction card about the strategies they use when trying to remember information.

WORDS ACTIVITY

Use the Words and Shapes Activities template included in this activity, (if you are in a Smart classroom, place them on the white board, if not place this information on two separate sheets of a flipchart or transparency.)

Make certain that you have a way to keep students from seeing the information until you are ready to uncover it in class. You need a watch or clock with a second hand that you can use in class. Ask students to have a pen and pencil ready but they cannot use them until you tell them to do so. Inform them that you are introducing the topic of memory and this exercise can assist them in understanding the factors involved with their recall.

Step 1: Show them the sheet with words; allow them to view it for 15 seconds. At the end of the time, cover the words and tell them to write down as many of the words as they can recall. After a minute or two, ask them the following questions:

- How many words were there?
- Which words do they believe most people recalled? Why?
- How did most people write down the information? (in the same chart form in which they were presented? In a sentence? in a picture?)

Can your students generate from this exercise the factors that lead to recall? Are they now able to suggest that recall can be enhanced by grouping, counting, repeating, reviewing, recording, seeing familiar patterns, noting the position, hearing/seeing the unusual, or spending time (15 seconds is not enough time).

Step 2. Now, do the same procedure with the shapes sheet. Give students 45 seconds to look at the shapes before covering them up and asking students to record everything they remember. Then ask students the same questions as before. Did your students view the task of viewing the shapes differently from viewing the words? Did they use more of the memory producing factors to recall this information? How did they change their way of organizing information? Reinforce the idea of organizational constructs.

How can you apply the factors that enhance memory to the way you cover information in your classes? Do you see a connection between the methods, frequency, and amount of time you spend on a topic and the ability for your students to recall it? What does this information suggest for a classroom that is focused on learning?

friends	**tire**	**on**
their	**Did**	**school**
my	**have**	**flat**
a	**to**	**way**
morning	**?**	**this**

WORDS AND SHAPES ACTIVITY

Chapter 6

Careers

I. **CHAPTER SUMMARY**

Learning outcomes for this chapter

LO 6.1   Identify your ideal job
LO 6.2   Analyze the best strategies for finding and getting a job
LO 6.3   Maximize job interviewing skills

Message to student

Among the most dynamic processes you will undertake in college relates to career exploration. The careers that exist today might well be obsolete tomorrow—therefore, a developmental approach that you can use throughout your life needs to be integrated into your skill set. Taking a variety of classes and becoming involved in diverse organizations is a good way to prepare yourself to act on ideas that truly matter to you.

You shouldn't assume that the title of a major will guarantee a job in a specific field, nor should you allow your interest in a particular major to serve as a limiting factor for the job you may eventually undertake. The skills needed for a satisfying career—writing, speaking, and communicating your message will be as important to your academic success as to your selection of a specific job. Creating space in your educational journey for internships, undergraduate research, campus jobs, service learning and international travel will provide a strong foundation for making a good decision about the world of work you will enter upon graduation.

Message to instructor

Every piece of data in *The Chronicle of Higher Education* or other publications about education, indicates that students associate attending college with obtaining a high paying job. One of your primary teaching responsibilities will be *to expand* the notion of job or career preparation within the broader context of earning a degree in higher education. Very few students recognize that the process for being tapped for a promotion, higher pay, or position of importance begins with every skill they learn throughout their lives. They should plan to visit the various offices that support the decision-making processes for students (academic advisors, counseling center, peer career support, career development centers, etc.) and your class assignments should encourage this interaction. Students need to identify support structures for making good decisions under sometimes stressful circumstances.

Because the world is increasingly interdependent, a well-developed global understanding is more important today than ever before when considering career development. In addition to international experiences found in a study abroad program, it is critical to introduce your students to language development. And finally, to truly prepare for the world of work, you can never overemphasize the importance of planning, whether it is for the selection of a semester's schedule of courses or determining how to complete an entire course of study online. Students of the future will have more resources and opportunities than ever before but they must be agile in their abilities to access the information needed to make their career happen.

II. KEY IDEAS AND CONCEPTS TO CONSIDER
Refer also to key terms listed in back of chapter.

resume
electronic portfolios
cover letter
internship
co-op experience
mock interview
informational interview
job interview
on-line career accounts
self discovery
career assessments
interest inventories
career research

III. CLARIFYING QUESTIONS AND DISCUSSION PROMPTS
At the end of each chapter in the Annotated Instructor's Edition (AIE), teaching tips, discussion prompts, student alerts and additional exercises and activities are organized around specific learning outcomes. These questions can be used to encourage class discussion, small group work, and/or individual reflection about the information presented in this chapter.

1. What are the resources at your institution that support career development? What populations do these different resources specialize in serving?
2. What kinds of job experiences have you had at this point in your life? Can you attach specific job-related skills to these experiences?
3. What qualities or characteristics do you associate with specific careers?
4. What attributes of a career do you view as being achieved only through the completion of a college degree?
5. What do you love to spend time doing? What passions do you have that you would like to integrate into your lifelong career?

IV. CLASSROOM ACTIVITIES AND ASSIGNMENTS
Consider using the following exercises when teaching this chapter. Always refer to the Instructor's Annotations at the end of each chapter in the AIE. Those listed below with an asterisk (*) can be found at the end of this chapter in Section VIII; those with a double asterisk (**) are in the student text. Others are self-explanatory.

Interview upperclassmen or recent graduates who have majored in or participated in specific academic experiences that are similar to those you would like to have. Find out how they made their decisions; which classes they found most valuable; what experiences made a difference.

*Interview faculty/staff/university employees in an area that interests you.

*Admit/Exit Cards (5–10 minutes, out of class); specifically ask students to discuss concerns about their career choices and the necessary course of study to obtain that career.

**TRY IT! 1 (20 minutes, in or out of class for initial assessment, followed by reflective thinking outside of class that leads to a four-line response)

V.   USING THE P.O.W.E.R. LEARNING PROCESS IN YOUR INSTRUCTION
Whether you are learning to learn or learning to teach, Bob Feldman's P.O.W.E.R. Learning process is a useful tool. Here are our ideas for applying this process as an instructor with this chapter.

P.repare: Assign TRY IT! 1 for your students to complete prior to class. Tell each student to come with the four-line descriptor of what their ideal job would involve. Arrange for your class to meet in a computer lab, career development center, job placement center, or library setting.

O.rganize: Using their four-line descriptor, have students interview fellow classmates and gather those with similar job descriptions into small groups (3–5 each).

W.ork: Working with your team, use current on-line or print resources that can be used to identify jobs or career fields that include the specific attributes that your team has decided are important.

E.valuate: Each group will present their findings to the class. Do you now have a broader or more narrow field of interest in a career or profession?

R.ethink: What courses will you now take? What experiences will you now attempt to include in your education?

TRY IT!   In the space below, begin a teaching journal of the ideas that worked and changes you would make the next time you teach this topic.

_____

_____

_____

VI.   CONNECTIONS WITHIN THE TEXT
       Consider bringing up this chapter's ideas again in the following contexts:

       Chapter 1   link goals for college and personal mission statement to this
                              chapter
       Chapters 2, 3, 4, 5   these are specific skills that will be used in virtually every
                              college graduate's career. Engage students in making the
                              most of this knowledge.
       Chapter 8   being able to make good decisions is critical to your success in
                              making solid career decisions.
       Chapter 10   making a career decision can be stressful; develop techniques to
                              cope with the side effects of stress.

VII.   CONTINUING THE CONVERSATION BEYOND THE CLASSROOM
       Creating opportunities for learners to become actively involved in the process of
       thinking, doing, and reflecting is a key role for the instructor. In addition to supporting
       the private dialogue between the textbook author and the student, you need to encourage
       students to share their thoughts with one another and with you, thus extending the
       conversation into the classroom setting. We believe that you must consciously connect
       the course content to
       • the individual student's life,
       • the broader academic community,
       • the world in which we live—our global society.

       Here are some ideas that can carry the conversation beyond the chapter activities.

GOAL: To connect the information to the individual student's life

       1.   Interview your parents. Ask them how they got their jobs. What was their job
              search like? Do you think that today's economic climate, access to technology,
              and mobile society have changed the process necessary for preparing for and
              finding a job?
       2.   Create the resume that you would like to give a potential employer when you are
              in the last year of your program. What types of courses and experiences (in and
              out of class) can you envision being able to include on this resume to get your
              perfect job?

GOAL: To connect the information to the broader academic community

       1.   Interview an instructor in a field that interests you. Ask why they chose to
              work in higher education instead of some other setting (corporate, non-profit,
              etc.). What non-teaching careers are possible in an educational setting? Would
              you be interested in exploring a specific profession (health care, law,
              architecture, business, etc.) within the context of higher education? Why or why
              not?

2. Contact the office or individual in your institution responsible for working with graduates and ask for the contact information of alums who are willing to answer questions about specific careers or who might sponsor internships or job shadowing opportunities.

3. Participate in a community or institution sponsored Career Day program.

GOAL: To connect to the global society

1. Have you ever considered that your education can be used to change the world? The Peace Corps, diplomatic service, and the military depend on educated people to make decisions and represent nations throughout the world. Check on your campus and see who has connected their academic experiences to one of these services.

2. Identify 3 potential programs and determine whether you can also travel abroad to meet course or internship requirements. When would you need to plan for this experience as an undergraduate?

3. Visit a library or go online and check out a foreign newspaper from a country you would like to visit (many have English editions); view the advertisements for jobs and see how many appeal to you.

4. Identify a recent opening or closing of a local industry. Uncover the reasons for this action and identify the connections you can attribute to a global economy.

VIII.   CLASSROOM ACTIVITIES TO SUPPORT TEACHING THIS CHAPTER
- Admit/Exit Cards
- Professor Interview
- Resume Power Words
- Career Planning Timeline
- What Job Am I?

ADMIT/EXIT CARDS

There are many variations on this idea. Consider which of these ideas appeal to you; mix and match ideas or create your own. Here are some examples:

1. To be admitted to class, students are told ahead of time that they must arrive with a question about the topic to be discussed that day. The teacher arrives early and collects the card with the question at the door. No card, no admittance.

2. In the syllabus, students are informed that they must write a 3–5 sentence paragraph responding to the prompt "Since the last class, I have observed or accomplished the following about my educational goals…." The card with this paragraph is due at the beginning of each class period and must include the student's name and the date. Not only does this promote reflective thinking about learning, but also it creates a private conversation between the faculty member and the student. Furthermore, the faculty member can use the cards to determine class attendance and, when the cards are returned, the student has a record of his/her attendance as well.

3. Students are requested to record what they have read since the last class (be it required or for pleasure) and to provide comments about their readings. Placed on a 3"× 5" card, with the student's name and date, this card is taken up at the beginning of each class.

4. At the end of each class, students have to provide a card in order to leave. Request your students to do one of the following:
   - write a summary of the day's lesson
   - write one question that has been left unanswered about the day's topic
   - make an observation about how today's lecture applies to another class
   - define a keyword that summarizes the lesson
   - critique the instructor's teaching
   - critique the student's participation
   - identify the "muddiest point" from the lecture
   - suggest the next class topic

PROFESSOR/STAFF INTERVIEW

Name _____ Person being interviewed _____
Date _____ Course _____

Please schedule an interview with one of your current professors or other employee of your institutional community and complete the following questions. Feel free to add questions of your own, but be respectful of this person's schedule.

1. How did you choose your particular field? How old were you when you decided to go into it? Did you ever want to do anything else?
2. Where did you go to school? What teacher had the greatest influence on you? Why? Did the influence impact your career choice?
3. What do you like best about teaching? What do you like least?
4. What do you hope students will understand about themselves when the semester is over? What transferable skills should they possess?
5. Do you have a philosophy of teaching?
6. What lifestyle factors were most relevant to your career choices? What challenges have existed by working on a college campus?
7. What do you believe are the greatest concerns facing first year students? Why do you think this? (If the person attended college)—What were your greatest concerns in your first year?
8. How would describe the ideal student?
9. What significant experiences beyond the classroom shaped your undergraduate years?
10. What do you do with your spare time?
11. If you had it to do over again, would you pursue the same profession? Why or why not?

POWER WORDS FOR YOUR RESUME

All resumes may look alike but they don't all read alike. Consider using any of the following verbs to describe your accomplishments when preparing your resume. Add to the list as you go through your career.

1. Go through the entire list and check off all of the action verbs (skills) employers in your intended career field look for.
2. Go through the list a second time and check off all of the verbs (skills) you have used in the experiences you are describing on your resume.
3. Note all of the words that you have checked twice and incorporate into your resume (and cover letters) the ones that best describe your skills and abilities.

accelerated	created	generated	medicated	reported
accomplished	defined	governed	modified	researched
achieved	delegated	graduated	monitored	reviewed
adapted	demonstrated	guided	motivated	revised
administered	designed	halved	negotiated	scheduled
advanced to	detailed	headed	obtained	served
advertised	developed	hired	operated	simplified
advised	devised	identified	ordered	sparked
analyzed	directed	illustrated	organized	sold
approved	discovered	implemented	originated	solved
arranged	distributed	improved	overcame	specified
assembled	doubled	increased	participated	stimulated
assisted	drafted	influenced	performed	strengthened
built	earned	informed	persuaded	structured
calculated	edited	initiated	pioneered	succeeded
changed	educated	innovated	planned	supervised
clarified	effected	inspired	prepared	surveyed
collaborated	eliminated	installed	presented	synthesized
collected	engineered	integrated	processed	taught
communicated	established	interpreted	programmed	trained
compiled	estimated	interviewed	promoted	transformed
completed	evaluated	invented	proposed	transmitted
composed	examined	investigated	provided	trebled
conceived	executed	justified	publicized	unified
conceptualized	expanded	keynote	purchased	used
conducted	experienced	led	reconciled	won
controlled	explained	licensed	recorded	wrote
converted	facilitated	maintained	recruited	wrought
coordinated	financed	managed	reduced	
constructed	formed	manipulated	reinforced	
consulted	formulated	marketed	related	
correlated	founded	mastered	reorganized	

A CAREER PLANNING TIMELINE

Don't wait until the last year of your program to think about career planning. There are steps you can take even if you haven't decided on a major when you first enter college.

Early in the your program
1. Visit a peer career center or other early career exploration site
2. Explore your interests and abilities by taking a variety of classes
3. Become involved in a student organization
4. Start your resume and career portfolio
5. Research careers
6. Visit the campus career development center
7. Explore leadership position and community programs
8. Seek out volunteer opportunities
9. Take a course with a service learning requirement
10. Update your resume and career portfolio
11. Take on assignments that relate to your career interests
12. Declare your major and map out your academic plan

Later in your program
13. Activate an online career account with your campus career development center or placement office
14. Identify an internship opportunity
15. Conduct informational interviews
16. Start networking
17. Become involved in professional associations
18. Work on career-related skill development
19. Update your resume and career portfolio
20. Refine your resume and career portfolio
21. Develop interview and job-seeking skills
22. Explore options for graduate study
23. Focus on career preferences
24. Network! Network! Network!
25. Start targeting employers
26. Conduct your job search

WHAT JOB AM I?

Jobs come in all shapes and sizes. Most students arrive at college with a fairly limited knowledge of the attributes associated with most jobs. Elements such as starting salaries, earning potential and work environments are shaped by the experiences of close friends and relatives or through television and books. This exercise is a fun way to start your students thinking about the job qualities they believe are essential for their happiness.

1. Identify the following characteristics for any one job—(nurse, bus driver, airline pilot, teacher, policeman, tax auditor, etc.)
   a. Starting salary
   b. 7 characteristics of the daily work environment (travel, work outside, meet with people, use up-to-date technology, lives of others depend on you, write reports, work with numbers, etc.)
   c. Average mid-career salary
   d. Long term earning potential
2. Ask all students to stand up. Without telling them what the job is, read out the different attributes, one by one. Tell the students to remain standing until they hear an attribute that they do not wish to have in a future job. After all of the attributes have been read, ask the students to guess what job you have just described. Sometimes students are surprised to learn that their ideas about different careers have been underdeveloped or overestimated.

Chapter 7

Technology and Information Competency

I.   CHAPTER SUMMARY

Learning outcomes for this chapter

LO 7.1   Explain the educational uses of technology
LO 7.2   Identify what is available on the Web
LO 7.3   Define distance learning
LO 7.4   Discuss how to develop information competency
LO 7.5   Explain what to keep in mind when using the Web to gather information

Message to the student

You have grown up in a world that is driven by technology and instant access to information. Many of you are computer literate and excited about using computers in your learning environment. But personal desk or laptop computers are not the only technological tools at your disposal—there are cell phones, smart phones pagers, DVDs, PDAs, mp3s, iPods, and digital cameras that are multi-purposeful. Some of these items can provide access to e-mail, text messages, Web blogs, books, articles, music, films, and pictures. Anything that can be digitized can be shared and surprisingly little cannot be digitized. It is useful to know both the abilities and limits of these tools so that you can make wise choices about the ones that can actually allow you to be more efficient and effective in your studies. In addition to identifying the tools that you are willing to use, you need to develop solid discrimination skills that allow you to gather accurate information and not waste time with poor resources. Others of you may not be as technologically savvy but are keenly aware of the urgency to learn more about how to negotiate learning in a virtual world. This chapter provides a solid introduction to the academic applications of technology that are appropriate for both novice and expert users.

Message to the instructor

While it is humbling to admit it, most faculty members are immigrants and most students are natives in the world of technology. A key issue in approaching this chapter is to assess the computing and library skills your students bring to the classroom. Furthermore, you need to know how your particular institution prepares and supports its students through technology. The learning and lifestyle choices influenced by our access to computers and other technological tools can be far reaching. Some students in your classroom may not have a home computer but virtually all of them have been to a high school with access to computers. Many of your students may have applied to your program through an electronic application, participated in a virtual tour of your institution, and even registered online for specific student services (e.g., parking permit, orientation, classes, etc.). Your institution may be one that requires students to create an electronic portfolio that can be evaluated easily by several individuals. No matter what differences and similarities exist among your students, you are truly doing them a disservice if you do not address this topic in your course. Despite your preferences and biases, individuals who can navigate change through technology will be the most successful. Also, as you attempt to build a supportive community among your students, you will want to encourage them to communicate regularly; technology makes this easier.

Beyond the technology, a numbing explosion of information occurred over the last quarter of a century. The amount is overwhelming and our response is often to be moved and seduced instead of thoughtful and questioning. Never has the ability to discriminate been more needed by our students. This chapter provides a wonderful platform for discussions about how to select sources that are credible and useful.

II. KEY IDEAS AND CONCEPTS TO CONSIDER
Refer also to key terms listed in back of the chapter.

assistive technology
Blackboard, WebCT, Moodle
blog
chat rooms
digital identity
electronic portfolio
electronic resume
Facebook, MySpace
Information Commons
information management
Instant Messaging
mp3 player
netiquette
personal data assistant (PDA)
podcast
Smart classrooms
text messaging
virtual classrooms
Wiki

III. CLARIFYING QUESTIONS AND DISCUSSION PROMPTS
At the end of each chapter in the Annotated Instructor's Edition (AIE), teaching tips, discussion prompts, student alerts and additional exercises and activities are organized around specific learning outcomes. These questions can be used to encourage class discussion, small group work, and/or individual reflection about the information presented in this chapter.

1 . On a scale of 1 to10 (with 10 being most proficient), how would you characterize your level of current proficiency with technology?
- E-mail?
- Instant messaging?

- Word processing?
- Internet or Web experience?
- Telephone?
- Text messaging?

2. Why does e-mail allow us to feel an anonymity that we should not?
3. Does this anonymity encourage uncivil behavior?
4. How would you characterize your current level of information competency/library skills?
    - Have you written a research paper?
    - What kinds of sources were you required to include?
    - What documentation formats are you familiar with?
5. How important will finding and using information be to you during the first year of your program?
6. What classes are you now taking that expect you to engage in research activities that will require technology?
7. Do any of your current courses include technology as part of the requirements? If so, how?
8. Do you maintain a profile on Facebook or MySpace? To what level are you willing to reveal personal information in a public domain? What are the implications of your choices with regard to such revelations?

IV.   CLASSROOM ACTIVITIES AND ASSIGNMENTS
Consider using the following exercises when teaching this chapter. Always refer to the Instructor's Annotations at the end of each chapter in the AIE. Those listed below with an asterisk (*) can be found at the end of this chapter in Section VIII; those with a double asterisk (**) are in the student text. Others are self-explanatory.

*Library Assignment
**Journal Reflections (15 minutes, in class)
**Try It! 3 (30–40 minutes, out of class)
**Try It! 5 (20 minutes, in or out of class)

V.   USING THE P.O.W.E.R. LEARNING PROCESS IN YOUR INSTRUCTION
Whether you are learning to learn or learning to teach, Bob Feldman's P.O.W.E.R. Learning process is a useful tool. Here are our ideas for applying this process as   an instructor with this chapter.

P.repare: Depending upon the needs of your particular class, plan on teaching this class period either in the library or in an electronic classroom or, if possible, in an electronic classroom in the library. If you have not already done so, establish a class e-mail distribution list or discussion board. Send a message to all of your students outlining the assignment discussed in the W.ork section. Your students can read this message during class when you teach or to check on their ability to use e-mail or the discussion board.

O.rganize: Have everyone in the class access any Web site that you know contains current, controversial material. You need to do this before the beginning of class. Pick one particular entry for the entire class to read.

W.ork: Ask students to access (and read) the Web site noted in O.rganize (above). Request your students to reply to your e-mail and the entire class. They should respond to one question regarding the validity of the article. True or not? Why or why not? In a mini-debate format, they should argue their position, pro or con with the entire class via e-mail.

E.valuate: Can the class evaluate their assessment of the Web site in light of the information presented in the chapter? What additional information would the class need to support or refute their position? Where would they find this information? Ask students to state the one important thing they learned about using information from this exercise.

R.ethink: Does this kind of applied exercise work with your class? If so, it can be a valuable tool for engaging the class in the hard work of practicing what we learn. If not, you may want to save this kind of exercise until the end of class, after the chapter has been discussed, or make an assignment for homework that students can bring to the following class.

TRY IT! In the space below, begin a teaching journal of the ideas that worked and changes you would make the next time you teach this topic.

_____

_____

_____

_____

_____

_____

VI.   CONNECTIONS WITHIN THIS TEXT AND YOUR CLASSROOM
       Consider bringing up this chapter's ideas again in the following contexts:

Chapter 1	link information about taking courses online to personal learning styles.
Chapter 2	link technology to time management; it can be a time saver or a "black hole."
Chapter 6	employers look for individuals with current technology skills and expect college graduates to know how to use technology in their communication and work.
Chapter 9	link issues of netiquette to getting along with others.

VII.   CONTINUING THE CONVERSATION BEYOND THE CLASSROOM
       Creating opportunities for learners to become actively involved in the process of thinking, doing, and reflecting is a key role for the instructor. In addition to supporting the private dialogue between the textbook author and the student, you need to encourage students to share their thoughts with one another and with you; thus, extending the conversation into the classroom setting. We believe that you must consciously connect the course content to

- the individual student's life,
- the programs and practices in the broader academic community,
- the world in which we live—our global society.

Here are some ideas that can carry the conversation beyond the chapter activities.

GOAL: To connect the information to the individual student's life.
       1.   Discover the e-mail address of someone you want to contact (a high school buddy, congressional representative, sibling).
       2.   Design a Web-based search that requires students to use online sources that address hobbies or personal interests.
       3.   Begin creating an electronic resume that can be submitted to individuals.

GOAL: To connect the information to the programs and practices in the broader academic community.

       1.   Give students a research assignment that explores the history and tradition of your university. If your institution holds a convocation or opening semester ceremony, use this event as a springboard for discussion about academic rituals and the celebration of educational values.
       2.   Imagine a classroom discussion that could take place over the Web in which race, gender, and/or physical disability might not play a role. What do your students think are the advantages and disadvantages of such a discussion?

3.   Well-developed service learning projects require students to prepare before experiencing the service work. Researching the problem that the service is expected to influence is a typical assignment. Connect this chapter to that work.

4.   If students are in a learning community or set of linked classes with a research project in one course, connect these skills to that expectation. Teach this chapter prior to or concurrently with the other faculty members to provide students with an understanding of the need to transfer skills from one course to another.

GOAL: To connect to the global society.

1.   Provide students with a Web-based assignment for exploring the possibilities of international study. Use the Web to discover five different ways they could travel abroad and continue earnings academic credit at your institution.

2.   Ask your students to find information about distance learning courses at an academic institution outside of the United States. Require them to bring the information to class for a discussion about the advantages and disadvantages of attending a school that they have never actually seen.

VIII.   CLASSROOM ACTIVITIES TO SUPPORT TEACHING THIS CHAPTER
   • Library Assignment

LIBRARY ASSIGNMENT

The central resource of any college or university is its library. University libraries are rich repositories of knowledge, ranging from printed books to ever expanding electronic information sources. Filled with the unexpected and open to the world, libraries offer intellectual liberation. Most importantly, once you have learned how to use the library effectively, you can quickly make use of any library in the United States. The organization of materials, the process for finding information, and the way to access material is almost always the same. Being able to find the information you need as a student, citizen, or person is a true mark of the educated person. A great deal, but not all, library information can now be accessed through computer searches, either in the library itself or from remote sites on campus, your personal computer, and around the world.

The purpose of the following activities is to assist you in understanding how to make the best use of our library. Additionally, it should provide you with a foundation for understanding the differences between a university library and a high school or hometown public library.

Can you answer the following questions?

PART I

1. **Circulation Desk: Its Function and Purpose**
   What do I need to check out a book?
   What is the lending period?
   How much is the fine each day a book is overdue?
   Can I check my own library account to see if books are overdue or if I have overdue fines? If so, how?
   Where can I make copies of materials?
   What is needed for making copies, and what is the process for doing so?
   What is interlibrary loan?
   What is the process for using interlibrary loan on our campus?

2. **Reference Desk**
   What can I learn here?

3. **Computerized Information Retrieval**
   What do I need to know to find a book in this library?
   Can I order an interlibrary loan book via computer?
   From which libraries do I have borrowing privileges on a regular basis as a result of attending this institution?
   What is the process for ordering these books or checking them out from those institutions?
   Why might I use a computer database with a printer searching for books?

4. **The Stacks**
   What are they, and where can they be found?
   How do I find a book on wellness that the library database tells me is in the library?
   Why is the Library of Congress system of cataloging books more widely used?
   Are any books catalogued using the Dewey Decimal System? If so, where are they kept?

5. **Reference Section**
   Where is this section, and how are materials organized here?
   Why are materials kept in this area?

6. **Periodicals Collection**
   Where is this section, and what is included here?
   How many periodical publications do I have in the library?
   How many periodical databases with full-text articles are available through an online collection?
   How do I locate periodical articles that are not available on the computer?
   Where are the hard copy periodical indexes?
   Can I use the computer to find newspaper articles? How?

PART II

On a separate sheet of paper, complete the following:

- Find and note the headline in the *New York Times* for the day you were born.
- Locate and print out (or copy down if the print function does not work) the call number, the title, author, publication date, and place of publication of one book pertaining to (*instructor's choice*—your group project, a personal interest, a class assignment, etc.) that is available in our library.
- Find, read, and write a one-page summary of one article pertaining to (*instructor's choice* – your group project, a personal interest, a class assignment, etc.) using the full-text databases or the bound periodicals.
- Find and note the title of one relevant reference book pertaining to (*instructor's choice*— your group project, a personal interest, a class assignment, etc.).

Chapter 8

Making Decisions and Problem Solving

I.   CHAPTER SUMMARY
     Learning outcomes for this chapter
     LO 8.1   Explain how to improve the quality of decisions
     LO 8.2   Identify strategies for problem solving
     LO 8.3   Analyze some programs that affect critical thinking and how to
                 avoid them

Message to the student
     Your first reaction to the title of this chapter is probably a very personal one. For
those of you who have just graduated from high school, you are probably on your own
for the first time in your life, and the decisions you are asked to make take on greater
meaning than before. Prior to college, you had family, friends, and community members
overseeing your decisions and providing reassurance or support for the choices you
made. You feel the weight of deciding about new friends, a new environment, and a new
lifestyle, but do you understand how your decision making affects your academic life?
Do you realize you have choices and there are different ways of arriving at those
decisions? For those of you who have been on your own and know the importance of
decision-making skills, what lessons have you learned that your classmates need to
know? How can you assist others in dealing with the luxury of choice?

Message to the instructor
     Too many students do not believe that they have control over their own destiny.
For many reasons (and you may want to explore these), many students today tend to
embrace the idea that things just happen to them. They don't feel in control and they
have learned to quickly make excuses, claim ignorance, blame others, pray for miracles,
or do anything rather than move internally to that difficult place called "personal
responsibility."
     Part of this concern results from the normal cognitive and emotional
developmental stage of younger students (17 or 18 years old). You need to assist them
in moving from a worldview that suggests that there is "a right or wrong answer" to one
that makes a place for many voices, solutions, and perspectives. The ability of students
to cope with this uncertainty is an indication of their maturation. For older and returning
students, taking on the new responsibilities of school in addition to work and family life
is a true juggling act. The decisions they make must account for the needs of others.
     This chapter provides the opportunity to hear that discussion in a less
emotionally charged arena by teaching the skills of good decision-making and problem
solving. This chapter provides you with an opportunity to revisit discussions about goal
setting and reinforce critical-thinking skills as you encourage your students to consider
alternatives and outcomes. And for this information to have lasting value for our
students, we must take that academic discussion and teach students how to apply those
skills to what Feldman refers to as "life's messier problems."

II.	KEY IDEAS AND CONCEPTS TO CONSIDER
	Refer also to key terms listed in back of chapter.

	decision making
	"life's messier problems"
	problem solving
	student development theory

III.	CLARIFYING QUESTIONS AND DISCUSSION PROMPTS
	At the end of each chapter in the Annotated Instructor's Edition (AIE), teaching
	tips, discussion prompts, student alerts and additional exercises and activities are
	organized around specific learning outcomes. These questions can be used to
	encourage class discussion, small group work, and/or individual reflection about
	the information presented in this chapter.

	1.	Have you made good decisions up to this point in your life?
	2.	Would the people who know you best (i.e., friends, parents, community members)
		say they trust your decision making?
	3.	What is the worst/best decision you have made in your life? What were the
		consequences/benefits?
	4.	Do friends/family come to you with problems to solve? Are you good at it?
	5.	What is the most difficult problem you have ever been involved in, and how did
		you resolve it?
	6.	What great decisions are facing you in college? What serious problems might you
		encounter?
	7.	How would you describe the process you use or the steps you take when making
		decisions?

IV.	CLASSROOM ACTIVITIES AND ASSIGNMENTS
	Consider using the following exercises when teaching this chapter. Always refer to the
	Instructor's Annotations at the end of each chapter in the AIE. Those listed below with
	an asterisk (*) can be found at the end of this chapter in Section VIII; those with a
	double asterisk (**) are in the student text. Others are self-explanatory.

	* Values Continuum (30 to 40 minutes, in class)
	* Locus of Control (20 to 30 minutes, in class)
	* Forced Choice activity (20 to 30 minutes, in class)
	** Career Connections (homework assignment, out-of-class)
	** Journal Reflections (admit card, 15 to 20 minutes, out-of-class)
	** Try It! 2 (20 minutes, in class)

Copyright © 2011 by The McGraw-Hill Companies, Inc.

V. USING THE P.O.W.E.R. LEARNING PROCESS IN YOUR INSTRUCTION

Whether you are learning to learn or learning to teach, Bob Feldman's P.O.W.E.R. Learning process is a useful tool. Here are our ideas for applying this process as an instructor with this chapter.

P.repare: Tell students to read Chapter 8 prior to class. Plan to open class with the Situation Box. This is an activity that will immediately pull your students into a conversation about making decisions. You'll need pencils, paper, and a box.

O.rganize: As students enter the room, hand out a piece of paper to each student. Stand in the middle of the room with the box in your hand—build a little suspense! After students are seated, announce the following task: Each student should write down one concern, question, or problem on their piece of paper and place it in the box.

W.ork: Every student in the class must draw a piece of paper from the box and facilitate a brief discussion about the situation, but only one situation should be drawn at the time. If everyone has their situation in their hands, they will be preparing their own ideas and they won't be listening! Students have the option of discussing the information on the paper or role-playing and presenting the problem, concern, or question in whatever way they choose. Preparation time should be limited to just a few minutes. The instructor should call time, bring a bell, a gong, or some "time device" to make it fun.

Now, ask the presenter to offer a response based on what they read in the chapter. Open the floor for other considerations. Allow three or four students to participate and then move on to the second student and the next selection from the box. Every time a specific strategy from the chapter is mentioned, write it on the board or on an overhead transparency.

E.valuate: Was this an effective way to teach this chapter? Were the students able to apply the decision-making and problem-solving techniques discussed in this chapter? How many strategies did the class generate? Refer to the board or overhead. Were you able to spot problems in the critical-thinking skills of your students?

R.ethink: Finding that hook to grab our students' attention and motivating them to turn that attention objectively on themselves is the key to success in teaching these skills. Will they approach a problem differently next time? Are they learning to accept responsibility and make better decisions?

TRY IT!   In the space below, begin a teaching journal of the ideas that worked and changes you would make the next time you teach this topic.

_____

_____

_____

_____

_____

_____

VI.   CONNECTIONS WITHIN THE TEXT
Consider bringing up this chapter's ideas again in the following contexts:

Chapter 1   link decision making to academic goal setting; refer to the MBTI or any other learning style inventory you conducted and discuss decision-making and problem solving in those terms; also, link to the personal mission statement.

Chapter 4   link decision making and problem solving to academic integrity.

Chapter 6   link decision making to the ability to manage the day-to-day tasks of a job. Also, as individuals move through their careers, they will often have an opportunity to make a decision to change jobs. The better their skills at making decisions, the less unsettling the changes will be.

VII.   CONTINUING THE CONVERSATION BEYOND THE CLASSROOM
Creating opportunities for learners to become actively involved in the process of thinking, doing, and reflecting is a key role for the instructor. In addition to supporting the private dialogue between the textbook author and the student, you need to encourage students to share their thoughts with one another and with you, thus extending the conversation into the classroom setting. We believe that you must consciously connect the course content to

- the individual student's life,
- the programs and practices in the broader academic community,
- the world in which we live—our global society.

Here are some ideas that can carry the conversation beyond the chapter activities.

GOAL: To connect the information to the individual student's life.

1. Family living situations demand a great deal of time. Ask students who live with families to identify strategies used at home to support academic success.
2. If most of your students live independently, dealing with the everyday dilemmas of paying rent, utilities, sharing resources and expenses fairly, commuting to campus, parking, and being in class on time provide rich ground for decision-making and problem-solving exercises.

GOAL: To connect the information to the programs and practices in the broader academic community.

1. This chapter provides an excellent opportunity to move your class out of the classroom and into the broader institutional community to explore career decision-making. Most institutions have career development centers or job placement offices that are wonderful resources. Connecting students to these resources will encourage use of those individuals and facilities.
2. Have the class brainstorm critical problems facing your institution—parking, growth, tuition increases, faculty hiring and firing policies, privacy issues concerning the use of e-mail, controversial speakers being invited to your campus, etc.—whatever issues your students will be drawn to. Have the students choose sides or research their positions and debate the issues in class. Instruct your students to focus on logical arguments and realistic solutions to the problems.

GOAL: To connect to the global society.

1. Just as there are hot topics on campuses, there are hotter ones in the global arena. The key here is to help students understand how international conflict, terrorism, global warming, deforestation, health crises, and other issues affect their world on a daily basis. Will our students choose to make these issues their own? Will they become world citizens or restrict their world only to those issues that impact their "backyard." This is the essence of becoming an educated human being, and it is our obligation as college instructors to give our students the intellectual courage to apply their knowledge beyond their doorsteps.
2. Another excellent opportunity to engage our students in global issues is through the use of a novel or other required reading in this course.

VIII. CLASSROOM ACTIVITIES TO SUPPORT TEACHING THIS CHAPTER
- Values Continuum
- Locus of Control
- Forced Choice

VALUES CONTINUUM

(Adapted from Katy Murphy's "Gaming: A Faculty Primer," presented at the FYE Conference in Columbia, South Carolina, February, 1995)

Students often believe that their classmates share their exact same values. This exercise provides a visual demonstration for your students to see where each member of the class stands on certain issues.

Step 1. The instructor creates five signs and places them on the wall around the classroom— STRONGLY AGREE, AGREE, UNDECIDED, DISAGREE, STRONGLY DISAGREE. This activity also works well as a "forced choice" event with an imaginary line in the middle of the room—one side is for "agree," the other "disagree."

Step 2. Students are told that the instructor will read a series of statements and students are to move to the sign that best reflects the opinion of the student. They are also informed that they must be able to discuss their reasons for standing in that area if called upon. It is important to remind students that there are no right or wrong opinions. Also, encourage them to be observant and respectful of differences.

Values Continuum Statements

1. Success is measured by how much money you make.
2. Parents should watch television with their children.
3. The greatest problem in the United States is too much individual freedom.
4. Abortions should be outlawed.
5. Computers in college labs should block access to Web sites with pornography.
6. The SAT is a good indicator of academic success in college.
7. The government should ban the use of tobacco and alcohol.
8. High school prepares students for the work they must do in college.
9. Requiring students to wear uniforms will solve many problems in public schools.
10. First year students should not be allowed to bring cars to campus.
11. Students should not be allowed to drop courses or change their schedules once classes have begun.
12. There is too much glorified violence in American movies.
13. College athletes should not be allowed to join a professional sports team until they have completed their college degree.
14. Handguns should be outlawed for anyone except police officers.

LOCUS OF CONTROL

(Adapted from Katy Murphy's "Gaming: A Faculty Primer," presented at the FYE Conference, Columbia, South Carolina, February, 1995)

It is a common tendency among first year college students to see outside forces as controlling their destiny. This activity allows students to express their feelings about control in areas that influence their lives. It could be important to acknowledge that the level of "control" we feel might change depending on our most immediate experiences. If a pattern of feeling "out of control" is felt with every topic, the student should take that as a serious warning. As with the Values Continuum exercise, this activity works well using a scale of one to five to reflect the level of control or as a simple forced choice exercise, with two possible choices: "Complete Control" or "Out of Control."

Procedure

Step 1. Place signs with one to five on the walls around the room or divide the room with one side designated as "Complete Control" and the other as "Out of Control."

Step 2. State the topic and let students move to the place in the room that best reflects their feelings. If appropriate, allow them to share their concerns.

Suggested Topics for Locus of Control Issues

Relationship with	**Class Assignments**	**Selecting a Major**
Parent(s) or family	**Health**	**Past Choices**
Money	**Eating Habits**	**Future Decision**
Time	**Sleep**	

FORCED CHOICE

"Thinking on your feet" is a skill that is valued in many environments; the Forced Choice exercise allows this to happen naturally. Create a list of eight to ten statements or questions on any topic; label one end of the room as Agree and the other end as Disagree. Pose the statement or question and have the students move to the appropriate side of the room. Allow one or two individuals to explain their choice without creating an opportunity for discussion. Then, quickly move on to the next question. This activity allows students to move around the room, to speak, and to listen.

Chapter 9

Diversity and Relationships

I.   CHAPTER SUMMARY
      Learning outcomes for this chapter
      LO 9.1   Explain why the increasing racial, ethnic, and cultural diversity of
                  society is important
      LO 9.2   Identify strategies to become more at ease with differences and diversity
      LO 9.3   Analyze how best to build lasting relationships and deal with conflict

      Message to the student
            You've probably had many people tell you that your college years will be the
      best years of your life. Or maybe folks told you that the friends you make in college
      would be your friends for years to come. But, did they prepare you for the joys and
      challenges that would come from being around so many individuals with different
      experiences, beliefs, and values from your own? Have you ever considered how you
      enter into your relationships? Most of life's enduring relationships take time, trust, and
      commitment. How long have you actually known the people you consider your friends?
      Relationships are dependent on the way you understand yourself and how you choose to
      interact and choose to include others you meet throughout your college years.

      Message to the instructor
            Regardless of your institution's location and characteristics—whether your
      campus is small and rural, large and urban, face-to-face or virtual, full of color and
      textures and difference of every sort, or seemingly homogeneous and predictable—it is
      important for you and your students to approach this chapter with an unbiased heart and
      mind. You must model the inclusion that is implicit in this chapter's discussion.
      Furthermore, you need to demonstrate an appreciation for both the individuality and
      diversity of your students. We all want to belong to some community; we want to share
      our stories, and we all must learn how to listen to others. Human relationships are
      powerful. As instructors, we want to teach the richness and the wonder of that power
      when used in positive ways.

II.   KEY IDEAS AND CONCEPTS TO CONSIDER
      Refer also to key terms listed in back of chapter.

      culture
      cultural competence
      diversity
      ethnicity
      humanity
      inclusion

multicultural
prejudice
profiling
race
respectful dialogue
stereotype

III.   CLARIFYING QUESTIONS AND DISCUSSION PROMPTS
At the end of each chapter in the Annotated Instructor's Edition (AIE), teaching
tips, discussion prompts, student alerts and additional exercises and activities are
organized around specific learning outcomes. These questions can be used to
encourage class discussion, small group work, and/or individual reflection about
the information presented in this chapter.

1. How would you define your cultural heritage?
2. Is that heritage all good or are there some things you wish were different?
3. How would you define diversity?
4. How important is it for you to be a part of a diverse community? Was it part of your
    thought process when you were choosing which college to attend?
5. Can you think of a defining moment in your life when you either a) discovered that
    you were different in some way or b) discovered or observed someone being treated
    differently from you?
6. What formal and informal ways has your campus sought to emphasize diversity?
7. What are the best things about human relationships in your life? What are the worst?
8. Are you a good communicator in your personal relationships?
9. How do you deal with conflict in relationship? What strategies have you used that
    worked well? What methods have you tried that failed?

IV.   CLASSROOM ACTIVITIES AND ASSIGNMENTS
Consider using the following exercises when teaching this chapter. Always refer to the
Instructor's Annotations at the end of each chapter in the AIE. Those listed below with
an asterisk (*) can be found at the end of this chapter in Section VIII; those with a
double asterisk (**) are in the student text. Others are self-explanatory.

*Admit/Exit Cards (5 to 10 minutes, out of class)
*What If? (30 minutes, in class)
* Multicultural Party (30 to 45 minutes, in class)
* Sexism? (45 minutes, in class)
* Parent Interview (45 minutes to 1 hour, out of class)
**Journal Reflections (15 minutes, in class)
**TRY IT! 2 (30 minutes, in class)

V. USING THE P.O.W.E.R. LEARNING PROCESS IN YOUR INSTRUCTION
Whether you are learning to learn or learning to teach, Bob Feldman's P.O.W.E.R. Learning process is a useful tool. Here are our ideas for applying this process as an instructor with this chapter.

P.repare: Role play is an excellent way to teach a chapter about getting along with others. Develop five to ten role play situations and write them on index cards. Sample topics might include:
- making friends
- communicating in relationships
- loneliness
- conflict (You could do all your role-playing on scenarios in this area; it is rich with possibilities.)
- changing relationships
- a friend in an intimate relationship with someone of a different race, religion, or ethnic group

Determine how many students are necessary to act out each scene and write that on the cards. *Special Note*: Student Affairs offices are generally a valuable resource for help in this area.

O.rganize: According to the number needed for each role-play, organize your class into groups and pass out the cards. Give students five to ten minutes to formulate their thoughts and plan their skit.

W.ork: All of your students should be working on pulling ideas together and coming up with a creative way to demonstrate their point. As each group presents, you must insist that all others listen actively. Have the listeners jot down their thoughts to be shared in an open-class discussion following each role-play. Students should be able to share what they observed, and perhaps what they would do differently.

E.valuate: As a homework assignment, ask students to write a reflection card answering the questions found in either "Evaluate: Checking Your Progress in Attaining Cultural Competence." These are excellent, thoughtful questions that should result in important statements regarding personal growth.

R.ethink: Your rethinking of the teaching of this chapter should be reflected in your comments on each student's paper. You may also want to use these papers as part of a closure activity for the class at the end of the semester.

TRY IT!   In the space below, begin a teaching journal of the ideas that worked
and changes you would make the next time you teach this topic.

_____

_____

_____

_____

_____

_____

_____

_____

VI.   CONNECTIONS WITHIN THE TEXT
Consider bringing up this chapter's ideas again in the following contexts:

Chapter 1	link relationships to learning preferences and differences
Chapter 6	link relationships to choosing a career as well as diversity needs in the business world
Chapter 8	link this chapter to decision making and problem solving
Chapter 10	link relationships to stress management

VII.   CONTINUING THE CONVERSATION BEYOND THE CLASSROOM
Creating opportunities for learners to become actively involved in the process of
thinking, doing, and reflecting is a key role for the instructor. In addition to supporting
the private dialogue between the textbook author and the student, you need to encourage
students to share their thoughts with one another and with you, thus extending the
conversation into the classroom setting. We believe that you must consciously connect
the course content to
- the individual student's life,
- the programs and practices in the broader academic community,
- the world in which we live—our global society.

Here are some ideas that can carry the conversation beyond the chapter activities.

GOAL: To connect the information to the individual student's life.

1. Living issues will abound in your discussion of this chapter—whether your students live in on campus or share an apartment or house with their families. Facilitate a discussion on living with others.
2. Ask students to consider their relationships with their parents, siblings, and family members. What about those relationships is positive? Negative? How do the relationship patterns they are creating now reflect the connections they already know with their families?
3. If you are using a novel or a film in your class, your assignments can focus on relationships between characters in the story. Ask students to identify healthy and non-healthy relationships and to analyze the factors involved. Then, have students compare these relationships to personal experiences.

GOAL: To connect the information to the broader academic community.

1. If your campus has an office for international studies, this is an excellent time to invite them to your class to explain the many options for study abroad. Perhaps you could include international students in this discussion.
2. Include a service-learning component as part of your course requirements. This is one of the best ways to teach students how to get along with others. Your institution may have a service-learning coordinator as a staff member or you may need to call on professionals in your town or county. The possibilities are endless and the rewards for you and your students are great.
3. Disability service programs provide an understanding of how a disability in one area can be an ability in another. Visit the campus office responsible for this program.

GOAL: To connect to the global society.

1. Any activity you plan that includes international studies (see above) will obviously connect your students to the global community. This is a theme you can develop throughout the semester, not just with this particular chapter.
2. While service-learning projects tend to be directed locally, they do provide a great connection to our global community. Looking at programs like AmeriCorps, Peace Corps, Teach for America, and internship possibilities in other countries all lead students to expand their sights on what they might envision for their futures. Web searches, campus interviews, and guest speakers are all rich possibilities for introducing this material.

3. Global interdependency is very relationship based. Ask your students to bring in examples of healthy and non-healthy relationship interaction between two or more countries. What would they recommend doing differently?

VIII. CLASSROOM ACTIVITIES TO SUPPORT TEACHING THIS CHAPTER
- Admit/Exit Cards
- What If?
- Multicultural Party
- Sexism?
- Parent/Spouse/Family Interview

ADMIT/EXIT CARDS

There are many variations on this idea. Consider which of these ideas appeal to you; mix and match ideas or create your own. Here are some examples:

1. To be admitted to class, students are told ahead of time that they must arrive with a question about the topic to be discussed that day. The teacher arrives early and collects the card with the question at the door. No card, no admittance.

2. In the syllabus, students are informed that they must write a three to five sentence paragraph responding to the prompt: "Since the last class, I have observed or accomplished the following about my educational goals…." The card with this paragraph is due at the beginning of each class period and must include the student's name and the date. Not only does this promote reflective thinking about learning but also it creates a private conversation between the faculty member and the student. Furthermore, the faculty member can use the cards to determine class attendance and when the cards are returned, the student has a record of his/her attendance as well.

3. Students are requested to record what they have read since the last class (be it required or for pleasure) and to provide comments about their readings. Placed on a 3 × 5 index card, with the student's name and date, this card is taken up at the beginning of each class.

4. At the end of each class, students have to provide a card in order to leave. Request your students to do one of the following:
   - write a summary of the day's lesson.
   - write one question that has been left unanswered about the day's topic.
   - make an observation about how today's lecture applies to another class.
   - define a keyword that summarizes the lesson.
   - critique the instructor's teaching.
   - critique the student's participation.
   - identify the "muddiest point" from the lecture.
   - suggest what the next class topic should or will be.

WHAT IF?

(Adapted from Katy Murphy's "Gaming: A Faculty Primer," presented at the FYE Conference, Columbia, South Carolina, February, 1995)

This activity promotes awareness of gender differences and allows your class to discuss stereotypes and biases. This is a focused Think/Pair/Share activity.

Procedure

Step 1. Distribute 3 × 5 index cards to each student. Instruct them to close their eyes and imagine that they wake up tomorrow as the opposite sex.

Step 2. Ask them to write eight to ten statements about how their life would be different (appearance, behavior, goals/dreams, eating habits, leisure activities, friends, etc.).

Step 3. Then, by each statement, they should put a "+" if it is a positive difference or a "–" if it is a negative difference.

Step 4. Discuss the statements first as pairs (preferably a male and a female). Then, discuss the findings as a class.

Step 5. How might this exercise assist your students in developing an understanding for someone who is transgender?

MULTICULTURAL PARTY

This is a simulation activity that truly sets the stage for a thoughtful classroom discussion about stereotypes and our basic assumptions about other cultures.

Procedure

Step 1. The instructor identifies a room large enough for the entire class to mill around and mingle and obtains enough mailing labels so that each student in the class will have one. On each mailing label, the instructor writes a descriptive phrase that could be interpreted as a stereotype such as, honors society nerd, fraternity member, sorority chick, black basketball player, lesbian, homosexual, white golfer, good-looking guy with a new red sports car, exchange student from Africa, exchange student from Tibet, student with a Mexican name, star athlete, student from a farm wearing brogans, African-American Chancellor's Scholar, physically disabled student, student with a learning disability, and any others you choose to create.

Step 2. In class, have your students close their eyes and you place a label on each student's forehead. Do not tell them what their label says and ask them not to tell each other what the labels say. After this task is complete, you may ask them to keep their eyes closed (or open, based on their comfort) so that you may instruct them of the following:

> *"This activity is a simulation. In order for us to have a fruitful discussion afterwards, your cooperative and thoughtful participation is requested. Thank you."*

Then, you can set the stage with this story:

"You are a new student on our campus and you heard that there will be a mixer for all new students at the Union on Friday night. You wouldn't ordinarily go to such a party because you don't like to go to parties alone. However, on this particular night, you decide to check it out because you heard some of your hall mates were going. When you arrive at the door, you are surprised to find that you do not know a soul there. Even so, you decide to stay and try to strike up conversations with different students based on your interpretation of their label. To do so, you know it is rude and unacceptable to simply walk right up to someone and tell them what their label is—we never do that in real life, do we?—so you speak to them using phrases and statements that indicate to them that you KNOW who and what they are. It is important to try to speak to as many people at the party as you can, giving them hints about themselves through your conversation without revealing to them what their labels say. As you begin to guess what your own label is, you should respond to questions and comments from that particular identity."

At this point, tell them that the party has begun and that they should begin to mingle.

Allow the party to last about eight to ten minutes. Listen and observe the comments, statements, and reactions produced by your students. If someone comes in late, allow this person to be a silent observer with you. In some cases, (large classes for instance) you might actually plan to have observer labels so that a few students can assist with this aspect; observers cannot talk to those students attending the party but they can (and should) listen in on conversations.

Step 3. Processing this activity is a vital aspect of this exercise. Do not start this activity unless you have enough time to talk about what happened at the party. It takes a minimum of 15 to 20 minutes to process this event.

Instruct your students to return to their seats and *without looking at their label* they should answer the following questions:

What label have you been given?
What clues helped you reach this conclusion?
Which clue was most useful?
How did you feel once you determined your identity?
Was it early or late in the party?
After you determined your identify, did you begin to "behave" differently to let others know what your label was?

Now, look at your label? Were you correct? Answer the following questions as a class discussion:

How do you feel?
What did you notice about the party?
What did you notice about the statements made to you and those you made to others?

What does this say to you about the positive and negative value of stereotypical labels?

Step 4. Wrapping up the activity. Things to notice, watch for, and/or comment on:
1. The longer the party lasts, the more flagrant and obvious people will become with their stereotypical remarks.
2. Once one person has created laughter with a stereotypical remark, the more likely others will try harder to create the same result.
3. Some students will withdraw and not enjoy the party because of the perception they have of themselves via the label.
4. Some students will find a group of "like" folks and quit talking via labels and try to carry on other types of conversation.
5. Some students may be uncomfortable accepting the idea that they do operate with generalizations about other groups or affiliations of people.

All of these responses and reactions are normal and can provide interesting points of discussion. The idea that we create much of our self-concept through the eyes of others is particularly important to acknowledge. In the end, we are what we tell ourselves we are and we tell ourselves what people around us tell us. It is critical to impress upon your students that we make people believe that they are intelligent, kind, peaceful, stupid, dirty, thoughtful, thoughtless, useful, useless, trustworthy, untrustworthy, etc.

As a teacher… it is extremely important to realize that our students often become what we tell them they are.

SEXISM/ SEXUAL HARASSMENT
(Katy Murphy, "Gaming; A Faculty Primer," presented at the FYE Conference, Columbia, South Carolina, February, 1995)

This activity—a case study discussion—opens a door to questions about sexism and sexual harassment. Case studies start interesting discussions because they present situations that are safe to talk about; they are someone else's story. Often, students in your class will have some personal experiences that are represented by the case study but seldom will a student be threatened by the idea that his or her story is the one being used.
This is often a hot topic on campuses and you probably have your own biases about what is acceptable and what is inappropriate. Be certain to have an up-to-date policy with institutional procedures available for your students OR invite your institution's legal counsel or student advocate to be a part of this class.

CASE 1

Dr. George Brown has been teaching at State College for over ten years. His discipline is English, specializing in Victorian literature. He utilizes both lecture and discussion in his classes.

Sharon Davis is a sophomore enrolled in Dr. Brown's literature class. She has heard a lot of positive comments from other students about Professor Brown and is looking forward to this course. Midway through the semester, Sharon has made several observations about Dr. Brown.

1. He calls on male students more than female students.
2. He interrupts female students when they are talking more than male students.
3. The course includes no women authors.
4. He addresses the students as "men and girls."
5. During student presentations Dr. Brown stares up and down when a woman is speaking.
6. In one of the books required for the course, the story involves a sexual relationship between a younger woman and an older man. During the class discussion, Dr. Brown asks each woman student if she would have an affair with an older man.
7. After receiving a C- grade on her first paper, Sharon goes by Dr. Brown's office for help. After sitting down to talk with him, Dr. Brown shuts his office door and invites Sharon out for coffee to discuss her grade. Sharon hesitates and Dr. Brown says, "I'm sure if we have a cup of coffee, it will help your grade."

Sharon, upset, leaves his office. She is too embarrassed to return to class and withdraws from the course. Of the seven situations Sharon observed, which, if any, are sexist? Which, if any, is sexual harassment?

CASE 2

Dr. Sally Fenslach has been teaching for eight years at Sacred Heart University. Her discipline is history, specializing in the medieval period. She utilizes both lecture and discussion in her classes.

John Dunn is a sophomore enrolled in Dr. Fenslach's history class. He has heard a lot of positive comments from other students about Professor Fenslach and is looking forward to this course. Midway through the semester, John has made several observations about Dr. Fenslach.

1. She calls on female students more than male students.
2. She interrupts male students when they are talking more than female students.
3. The supplemental readings for the course focus on the homosexual relationships for both men and women in the religious context.
4. She addresses the students as "women and boys."
5. During student presentations Dr. Fenslach smiles when women are speaking and looks down at her papers when a male student speaks.
6. After one of the books required for the course is discussed, Dr. Fenslach asks each student to share what they think about homosexual relationships among individuals in religious orders and to write a paper regarding contemporary beliefs and practices regarding the same. She goes on to suggest that students should include any personal homosexual experiences they have had with members of religious orders.
7. After receiving a C- grade on his paper, John goes by Dr. Fenslach's office for help. After sitting down to talk with her, Dr. Fenslach suggests that John did not include any personal homosexual experiences in his paper and thus, it did not

fulfill the assignment. John responded that he had not had any homosexual relationships. Dr. Fenslach looked at John with skepticism and told him then, the grade would have to stand as it was.

Of the seven situations John observed, which, if any, are sexist? Which, if any, is sexual harassment?

PARENT/SPOUSE/FAMILY INTERVIEW

Listening is perhaps the most important communication skill we can develop. The purposes of this interview are:

- to provide an opportunity for students to communicate with family members about their first several weeks of a term
- to give students a chance to find out how things may have changed for them and their families since beginning their educational program
- to increase the awareness of the need for continued family support and communication
- to promote the importance of developing listening skills

PARENT/SPOUSE/FAMILY INTERVIEW QUESTIONNAIRE

Student Name _____   **Parent(s) Name(s)** _____
                                                                                     _____

TIME REQUIRED: It takes approximately 20 minutes for the interview and another 15 minutes for writing reflections.

DESCRIPTION OF PROCESS: Each student will interview his or her family at home; let individuals know ahead of time you want to do this interview; pick a mutually convenient time and a comfortable setting (which could be the family room, kitchen table, back porch, etc.) that is free of distractions (no TV, no phones, no sibling interruptions, etc.). Ask the questions on this sheet, writing down the responses.

BEFORE YOU TURN IN THE QUESTIONNAIRE, write answers to the more general questions and be prepared to discuss your responses in class, if you are comfortable doing so.
Where is this interview being held?   _____

What is the time and date?   _____
1.   Please try to recall and describe your feelings when I started my educational program.

2.   What are the three most noticeable changes around the house since I started college?
        a. _____

        b. _____

        c. _____

3.   What were your impressions of my school when you first saw it?

4.   Do you think I have changed since I began college? If so, how? If not, what do you think might happen that will change me?

5.   What (seriously!) do you expect my grades to be this semester? Will it be okay if I don't make all A's? Do you have a specific grade point average that you expect?

6. What between us has changed? How much have we communicated since school started?

STUDENT IMPRESSIONS (ESSAY):
In the space provided, write up your impressions of the interview. Did you get any non-verbal cues from your guardians during the interview? Did you sense that your relationship has changed, and if so, how? Did the interview lead to more general discussions between you and your parents? If so, on what topics? How did the rules around the house differ this time? Were there matters that you did not feel comfortable talking about with your parents? What is one thing you learned from this conversation?

Chapter 10

Juggling: Stress, Money, Family and Work

I.   CHAPTER SUMMARY

Learning outcomes for this chapter

LO 10.1   Define stress and explain how to control it
LO 10.2   Explain what is involved with keeping fit and healthy
LO 10.3   Analyze the purpose for a budget and explain how to prepare and
          stick to one

Message to student

     School is not for wimps. Pursuing a college degree or program certificate is not only mentally challenging but also physically and emotionally demanding. Some of you have unlimited freedom of choice regarding when to eat, sleep or exercise. Others will be constrained in your choices by family or work obligations. Career opportunities, lifestyle options, and long-term financial security will be tied to many of the decisions you make while you are a student. You have the freedom to choose with whom you associate; the manner in which you develop and maintain personal relationships can influence your overall emotional and physical well-being. You may have illnesses, disabilities, or experience loss over which you do not have control but your responses and attitudes about these aspects of your life are totally within your control. Opportunities for creating debt abound. Additionally, you will have tremendous influence over the choices that family members, classmates, and friends make. When you know that someone is making unwise or unhealthy decisions, it is incumbent upon you to speak up. This chapter explores the role that competing influences in your life play and provides you with honest, appropriate information that should be taken to heart as you consider the lifestyle choices and habits that will serve you as a student and beyond your college experience.

Message to instructor

     Leading your students through conversations about making choices that enhance their health requires trust and respect. As a result, this chapter is not easily taught in the beginning of the semester, even though that is when it seems that our students need and would benefit most from it at that time. It simply makes sense that you need to develop a relationship with someone before discussing eating habits, rest, addictions, money or other issues related to personal choice. ***At the very least, it is critical for you to emphasize the need to develop a culture of concern for one another.*** Each individual has a responsibility to make healthy and wise choices but the safety of all requires that we watch out over one another as each of us learns to live well individually. Perhaps it is useful to know that by the middle or the end of the semester, there often (sadly) exist experiences and crises that make this information useful, even urgent. Many of them have seen or experienced first hand the outcomes of uneven availability of health care. Use current events to discuss issues of fiscal integrity and judicious financial planning. Our students have grown up in a world of financial scandal and imprudence. Is this the world they want future generations to know? You can expect some unusual revelations with your students when they begin to explore this information with you. Be genuine with your concern, thoughtful with your responses, and accurate with your referrals.

II. IDEAS AND CONCEPTS TO CONSIDER
Refer also to key terms listed in back of chapter.

barter system
budget
credit cards
financial aid
diet
disease
eating disorders
exercise
healthy relationships
stress
tobacco use
respect
revolving credit
virtual cash

III. CLARIFYING QUESTIONS AND DISCUSSION PROMPTS
At the end of each chapter in the Annotated Instructor's Edition (AIE), teaching tips, discussion prompts, student alerts and additional exercises and activities are organized around specific learning outcomes. These questions can be used to encourage class discussion, small group work, and/or individual reflection about the information presented in this chapter.

1. What causes personal and/or academic stress in your life?
2. How would you define health?
3. What habits would you like to change? How can you do this?
4. What would your day look like if you were to live a healthy life?
5. What role does your ability to maintain positive relationships play in your ability to remain healthy?
6. How are your personal values reflected in your lifestyle choices which affect your health?
7. What is the difference between a want and a need?
8. How do you justify the cost of higher education in your life? Is this the same motivation for all of your classmates?
9. Have you ever lived on a budget?
10. What sense do you have of the amount of money you need to live the way you believe you want to live? What starting salary (really) do you believe is appropriate at your first job out of college?

IV.   CLASSROOM ACTIVITIES AND ASSIGNMENTS
Consider using the following exercises when teaching this chapter. Always refer to the Instructor's Annotations at the end of each chapter in the AIE. Those listed below with an asterisk (*) can be found at the end of this chapter in Section VIII; those with a double asterisk (**) are in the student text. Others are self-explanatory.

*Admit/Exit Cards (5 to 10 minutes, out of class)
*Forced Choice (20 minutes, in class)
*Ways of Saving Money (10 minutes, in class)
*The Cost of Higher Education (20 minutes for research, in or out of class; 15 minutes to discuss Step 4, in class)
*Using Films in the Classroom (20 to 45 minutes, in class)
*Symbolic Gifts (1 to 2 hours, out of class; 45 minutes to an hour to discuss in class), an opportunity to show appreciation for what has been learned
*Good-Bye Cards (45 minutes to an hour, out of class, 5 minutes to distribute in class)
*Hot Seat (45 minutes to an hour, in class)
**TRY IT! 1 (15 minutes, in class)
**TRY IT! 2 (20 minutes, in class) this is a great brainstorming exercise

V.   USING THE P.O.W.E.R. LEARNING PROCESS IN YOUR INSTRUCTION
Whether you are learning to learn or learning to teach, Bob Feldman's P.O.W.E.R. Learning process is a useful tool. Here are our ideas for applying this process as an instructor with this chapter.

P.repare: Decide which topics your students would like to explore regarding health. Based on the chapter topics and individual student interests, make a list of possible topics and then ask your students to select the two to three areas about which they would like to learn more. Don't be shy about including topics you are concerned about or want to be certain to discuss.

O.rganize: Many campuses have individuals, groups, or organizations that regularly provide programs focusing on healthy lifestyles. Learn what is available on your campus. Often these speakers are in high demand and need one to two weeks notice before coming to your class. Make appropriate arrangements for your speaker that may include audio-visual equipment.

W.ork: Prior to the guest speaker's arrival, encourage your students to ask questions or to consider what they want to know about the expertise that the speaker might have. Have your students write these questions down on 3 × 5 index cards (without their names on them). They should look on the Web sites and find out as much information as possible prior to creating their questions so that they are able to gain new knowledge from the speaker. You should then provide the speaker with these cards/questions prior to the scheduled presentation.

E.valuate: Following the research, creation of questions, and presentation by the outside speaker, ask your students to write a reflection paper regarding healthy lifestyles. What about their lifestyle supports their pursuit of a college degree and what does not? What do they want to change, and how can they do it?

R.ethink: Now, what questions do they have about reducing stress or improving their health? What more do they want to know or need to know? Are there offices on campus that your students need to consider visiting outside of class? Are there programs or offices that need to be created on your campus because nothing more is available? Ask your students to explore these questions.

TRY IT!   In the space below, begin a teaching journal of the ideas that worked and changes you would make the next time you teach this topic.

_____

_____

_____

_____

_____

_____

_____

VI.   CONNECTIONS WITHIN THE TEXT
Consider bringing up this chapter's ideas again in the following contexts:

Chapter 1   link goals for college and personal mission statement
Chapter 2   connect the ability to make good choices about how to spend time
               to making good choices about how to spend money

Chapter 6   salary is only one consideration when determining a career path.
              Assist your students in understanding the value of intrinsic rewards
              in the context of job satisfaction
Chapter 9   budgeting is about making good decisions

VII. CONTINUING THE CONVERSATION BEYOND THE CLASSROOM

Creating opportunities for learners to become actively involved in the process of thinking, doing, and reflecting is a key role for the instructor. In addition to supporting the private dialogue between the textbook author and the student, you need to encourage students to share their thoughts with one another and with you, thus extending the conversation into the classroom setting. We believe that you must consciously connect the course content to

- the individual student's life,
- the programs and practices in the broader academic community,
- the world in which we live—our global society.

Here are some ideas that can carry the conversation beyond the chapter activities.

GOAL: To connect the information to the individual student's life.

1. Health concerns of American college students are often very different from those of the rest of the United States. An interesting and rather eye-opening assignment is to have your students research the health concerns of individuals who are not attending college and thus not living the very privileged life that you and your students live. How is it that individuals (you and your students) who have almost unlimited freedom of choice regarding diet, exercise, and access to health care sometimes choose to practice unhealthy lifestyles?

2. What habits do your students have that they can relate to their own family's practices? As they examine their habits, which ones would they want to keep when raising children of their own? Which ones would they discourage?

3. Ask students to write a paper or hold a class discussion about the following question: What role does advertising and a virtual 24-hour society play in supporting healthy or unhealthy lifestyle choices?

4. Saying good-bye is a difficult yet, critical aspect of living a healthy lifestyle. Use a series of film clips with the endings of several popular films as a way to illustrate this point. Not only do these commonly shared images provide our culture with ways to say good-bye but also this experience sets the tone for ending this course.

5. Encourage your students to look at the personal and academic goals they wrote during the earlier chapters of this book. Ask them to put a dollar amount by each goal. In class, ask them to discuss how they arrived at these figures. Based on this, how can they prepare for or meet their needs?

6. Remember the time management exercises? Use the same tools to develop money management skills. Ask your students to brainstorm all of the ways they can save money.

GOAL: To connect the information to the programs and practices in the broader academic community.

1. Have your students survey your campus for healthy and unhealthy services. Do snack machines have only high fat, high calorie items? Do drink machines have juice and water choices? Are there water fountains on each floor of each campus building? Are individuals encouraged to walk rather than drive on your campus? As a service-learning project, have them create an ideal healthy campus environment. They can share their ideas with one another or submit them to appropriate campus representatives who can implement these ideas. Consider putting this information on the Web.

2. Ask your students to create a program about health or campus safety that they would be willing to present to other students on your campus. It would be particularly useful for them to identify information that is not currently provided through an office or other organization.

3. Ask your students to identify the tool or idea that they learned about during this class that made the biggest difference in their ability to live in a healthy manner during the semester. They should bring in an object that symbolizes that idea (i.e., if time management was the most important idea, the object could be a broken watch). Ask them to leave that object with you so that at the start of next year's class, you may hand each new student "a gift of success" from those who came before them.

4. Have your students create a realistic budget to suggest for next year's first year students on your campus—this could be a service-learning project. Allow them to work in small groups and present this information to each other and create a pamphlet (suitable for distribution) outlining their suggestions and ideas for future students. Have them provide this information to the admissions office and/or financial aid office for informing future first year students.

5. Create small teams of students and assign a specific student service to each team such as tutoring, residence life, student union, and programs. Have these different teams meet with the director of these services and learn about the budgeting process involved in providing these services. Request that your students explore how various program budgets reflect or do not reflect values outlined in the institutional mission statement.

GOAL: To connect to the global society.

1. Americans, in general, have access to health care at a different level than the rest of the world. Ask your students to examine one culture that attempts to provide greater access to health care for its citizens and one that provides less access. What impact does this have on the overall health and well being of its citizens? What about longevity of life?

2. Some diseases are not only health concerns but also political and geographical issues. Ask your students to explore HIV/AIDS, polio, and tuberculosis through the filter of politics, religious beliefs, and ethnicity.
3. Ask students to consider the budgets of three different countries. Compare and contrast the financial commitments of these countries with regard to education, defense, and the environment. What values are reflected by the budget decisions of these countries?
4. Determine the "value" of a dollar in three different countries. Ask students to explore the cost of their most recent grocery bill from the perspective of a working citizen in each of those three countries.

VIII.   CLASSROOM ACTIVITIES TO SUPPORT TEACHING THIS CHAPTER
- Admit/Exit Cards
- Forced Choice
- Ways of Saving Money
- The Cost of Higher Education
- Using Films in the Classroom
- Symbolic Gifts
- Good-Bye Cards
- Hot Seat
- Short Relaxation Techniques
- Living on a Budget in College

ADMIT/EXIT CARDS

There are many variations on this idea. Consider which of these ideas appeal to you; mix and match ideas or create your own. Here are some examples:

1. To be admitted to class, students are told ahead of time that they must arrive with a question about the topic to be discussed that day. The teacher arrives early and collects the card with the question at the door. No card, no admittance.
2. In the syllabus, students are informed that they must write a three to five sentence paragraph responding to the prompt: "Since the last class, I have observed or accomplished the following about my educational goals…." The card with this paragraph is due at the beginning of each class period and must include the student's name and the date. Not only does this promote reflective thinking about learning but also it creates a private conversation between the faculty member and the student. Furthermore, the faculty member can use the cards to determine class attendance and when the cards are returned, the student has a record of his/her attendance as well.
3. Students are requested to record what they have read since the last class (be it required or for pleasure) and to provide comments about their readings. Placed on a 3 × 5 index card, with the student's name and date, this card is taken up at the beginning of each class.

4. At the end of each class, students have to provide a card in order to leave. Request your students to do one of the following:
   - write a summary of the day's lesson.
   - write one question that has been left unanswered about the day's topic.
   - make an observation about how today's lecture applies to another class.
   - define a keyword that summarizes the lesson.
   - critique the instructor's teaching.
   - critique the student's participation.
   - identify the "muddiest point" from the lecture.
   - suggest the next class topic.

FORCED CHOICE

"Thinking on your feet" is a skill that is valued in many environments; the Forced Choice exercise allows this to happen naturally. Create a list of 8 to 10 statements or questions on any topic and label one end of the room as "Agree" and the other end as "Disagree." Pose the statement or question and have the students move to the appropriate side of the room. Allow one or two individuals to explain their choice without creating an opportunity for discussion. Then, quickly move on to the next question. This activity allows students to move around the room, to speak, and to listen.

WAYS OF SAVING MONEY

This is a simple brainstorming activity that can enlighten not only your students but also can give you new ways to save money!

Procedure

Step 1. Ask students to work in small groups (three to five each) and come up with their top ten (realistic) ways of spending too much money in your particular town on a regular weekend. Give them large sheets of paper or poster board and have them write their ideas down—in descending order ten to one.

Step 2. Ask each group to then announce them (David Letterman style) to the rest of the class. Post these ideas around the room.

Step 3. Return to group work and ask your students to brainstorm as many ways as they can think of to spend less money. Encourage them to think differently and creatively (such as "make less money and I will spend less money"). You might also want them to make a list of "free or nearly free" entertainment available at your institution or in your town. Ask them to record all of their suggestions.

Step 4. Report out the ideas. Ask two students to record the suggestions and make a huge list of "ways to save money" and hang it in the classroom so that they can all be reminded on a regular basis how to save their dollars.

THE COST OF HIGHER EDUCATION

A simple way to enlighten students concerning the value of their money is by illustrating the cost of a college education. Use this activity to have students come up with the true investment they are making in college.

Procedure

Step 1. Have students figure out how much it actually costs per year to attend school. Encourage them to add in all of the costs, even if there is not a category (such as study abroad). They should determine what their total expenses would be throughout an entire undergraduate experience (four, five, or even six years).

Step 2. Next, ask your students to do a Web search of starting salaries of two types of jobs: those requiring an undergraduate college degree and a typical job (usually minimum wage) that does not require an undergraduate degree. Multiply each salary type by 30 years of employment (just arrive at the gross number, do not try to adjust for raises, benefits, increase in minimum wage, inflation, or deductions for taxes, insurance, etc.)

Step 3. Subtract the cost of an undergraduate education from the gross amount of working for 30 years in a job requiring such an education. Then compare that to the total amount earned if the student simply went to work and did not earn an undergraduate education.

Step 4. Ask them what they have discovered. Are they making an investment in going to college? Are they likely to earn more over a lifetime with a college degree than without one? How much of an investment in their future financial security is their degree?

USING FILMS IN COLLEGE CLASSROOMS

Films are extremely appropriate to use in college classrooms and can often illustrate a point better than your words and actions. Consider using films for any of the following reasons:

1. promote discussion about a value or theme relevant to college life and your course
2. provide a source of information for your students to practice listening skills concentration skills, note taking skills, or other study skills
3. accommodate students with different learning styles
4. appeal to students who have grown up in a multimedia culture

Be cautious about using films that are "dated" through dress or language unless you are willing for those elements to override the message you want your students to hear. Ask your colleagues and former students to assist you in creating a list of films that meet your needs. Take the time to view these films before showing them so that you can be prepared to address sensitive issues.

A particularly impressive way to use films in the classroom is through contemporary good-bye images. By showing the endings to several popular or well-known movies *(Big Fish, ELF, Garden State, Titanic, Lord of the Rings, Casablanca, etc.)* you can set the stage for a powerful discussion of what it means to say good-bye. It provides a fitting end for reviewing and evaluating what the class has done and what your relationship as a group means.

SYMBOLIC GIFTS

This activity can be used to provide closure to a class while reviewing what each person has learned. The task needs to be assigned at least one week before it is due.

Procedure

Step 1. Ask students to think about the most important factor they have learned that leads to student success. It can be done in conjunction with a specific course topic (health/wellness, time management, studying, etc.) or with regards to the entire semester. Tell them that each member of the class must prepare a fantasy "gift" that represents an object, value, person, or idea, and so on, of their choice that best leads to student success. The gift, due in a week, must be a tangible symbol that can be left behind. It should not be an expensive, irreplaceable, or perishable representation of the concept. In addition to the symbolic gift, they should have a one-page paper explaining the relationship between the gift and student success that they can hand in with the gift. Finally, they will be asked to briefly summarize (not read their paper) what their gift represents and why they believe it leads to student success. Inform them that the "gift" will be given to students enrolled in the next student success course that you teach. (An example, from a past class, was a broken watch that represented the importance of developing good time management skills.)

Step 2. On the due date, students ceremoniously present their gift to you and the class. Create a "fountain of gifts" in the front or center of the room. Use this exercise as an illustration of how we are responsible not only for learning but also for sharing with others what we have learned.

Step 3. Keep these gifts in your office and make a point of handing them out to your new students on the first day of class the next time you teach a student success course. Do not reveal the meaning behind the symbolic gift. Encourage your new students to simply accept this gift from those who have come before them. Allow them to ponder its significance. And be certain to repeat this exercise at the end of their semester.

GOOD-BYE CARDS

This activity involves each student writing a note to all other students in the class expressing their thanks, thoughts, or wishes for that person. This takes about 40 minutes in class (with a class of around 20 students). Faculty members should encourage students to read these notes immediately and then put them away to be read later. This final personal expression is a powerful way for students to remember each person in class.

HOT SEAT

This is a sharing activity designed to reinforce a sense of community, mutual trust, caring, and lasting communication. It can be used to confront a person about a health issue, to bring closure to a class, or to publicly praise one another. The instructor sets a serious, thoughtful tone for this exercise, encouraging everyone to remain involved and honest in his/her participation.

Procedure

Step 1. The class sits in a circle with a chair (swivel is preferable) in the center. Each student is invited to sit in the chair—the hot seat.

Step 2. Members of the class are then instructed that they have exactly two minutes (as a whole group) to share an important word (adjective) or phrase about that person with the goal of those few words conveying hopes and observations that will serve as a powerful closure to the course. It is useful to give a specific prompt such as:

Complete the following sentence about the person in the hot seat…
"I would like for you to become a healthier person by ……." or
"When I think about you, the following word or phrase always enters my mind… " or
Some prompt of your own creation.

The person in the hot seat should turn and look at whomever is speaking throughout this exercise. The instructor must keep time on this exercise and be strict about it or towards the end, you will not have enough time to complete the activity.

Step 3. After the two minutes is over, stop the answers. The only response allowed by the person in the hot seat is a simple: "Thank you." This person returns to his or her seat and another person is allowed to move into the center chair.

Extroverts will generally volunteer first, but eventually even the quietest and most reserved member of the class will step forward. The experience may be most powerful for those who wait to the last so don't let anyone off or hurry the final participants. Also, don't forget to take your own turn in the hot seat. This is a valuable feedback and closure activity.

SHORT RELAXATION TECHNIQUES

1. **Deep Breathing**
Slow your breathing, inhaling as deeply and slowly as comfortable, with your right hand on your abdomen. As you exhale, slowly say silently to yourself the phrase, "release, rest, and relax." Each time you exhale, breathe more slowly and more deeply. Each time you exhale, repeat the phrase. Allow your diaphragm to do all of the work. If the diaphragm is doing the breathing work, the hand on your abdomen should be the only other part of you that moves. (This may take some practice.)

2. **Quick Muscle Tensing**
Tense every muscle group in your body. Hold your breath and hold the tension while you slowly count to five. Then, relax and exhale. Take several slow, deep breaths, and then tense again. Allow yourself at least 30 seconds to enjoy the resulting feeling of relaxation.

3. **Quiet Reflection**
Take several deep breaths. Relax muscle tension. Imagine briefly a place that is very relaxing, safe, and comfortable. Visualize yourself in this safe and relaxing place. Notice the details of your surroundings—the objects close to you and those farther away. Notice the colors around you and the lights and shadows. Be aware of the time of day. Notice the textures—the feeling of the surfaces you are standing or sitting on, the way your clothing touches your skin, and the air moving against your skin. Allow your thoughts to slow down. Allow your mind to clear. When you are refreshed and ready to return to your activity, do so gradually.

LIVING ON A BUDGET IN COLLEGE

The following activity sheet can provide students with a concrete understanding of how much it costs to attend college.

Living on a BUDGET in College

Anticipated INCOME $_____
(all sources—parents, savings, job, scholarships, etc.)
Anticipated EXPENSES
    Tuition
    Fees   _____
    Room   _____
    Board   _____
    Other food   _____
        (vending machines, weekend pizza, coffee, etc.)
    Transportation   _____
        (going home and getting around locally)
    Parking
    Books   _____
    Phone   _____
    School supplies   _____
        (disks, network connection, pens, paper, etc.)
    Leisure/Pleasure Activities   _____
        (concert tickets, sports events, etc)
    Clothes
    Presents (birthday, holiday gifts, etc.)   _____
    Mail   _____
    Personal toiletries   _____
    Other (childcare, etc.)   _____

EXPENSE TOTAL $ _____
INCOME TOTAL $ _____
DIFFERENCE $ _____